How

COLES NOTES

Key Point

Basic concepts in point form.

Close Up

Additional hints, notes, tips or background information.

Watch Out!

Areas where problems frequently occur.

Quick Tip

Concise ideas to help you learn what you need to know.

Remember This!

Essential material for mastery of the topic.

COLES NOTES

Getting Along in . . .

Italian

For travellers

and students

Useful phrases

with pronunciations

Travel & culture tips

ABOUT COLES NOTES

COLES NOTES have been an indispensable aid to students on five continents since 1948.

COLES NOTES now offer titles on a wide range of general interest topics as well as traditional academic subject areas and individual literary works. All COLES NOTES are written by experts in their fields and reviewed for accuracy by independent authorities and the Coles Editorial Board.

COLES NOTES provide clear, concise explanations of their subject areas. Proper use of COLES NOTES will result in a broader understanding of the topic being studied. For academic subjects, Coles Notes are an invaluable aid for study, review and exam preparation. For literary works, COLES NOTES provide interesting interpretations and evaluations which supplement the text but are not intended as a substitute for reading the text itself. Use of the NOTES will serve not only to clarify the material being studied, but should enhance the reader's enjoyment of the topic.

COLES PUBLISHING. A division of Prospero Books

Toronto - Canada

Printed in Canada

Cataloguing in Publication Data

De Luca, Elena, 1951-

Getting along in—Italian

(Coles notes)

ISBN 0-7740-0574-2

1. Italian language—Conversation and phrase books—English.

I. Title. II. Series.

PC1121.D44 1998 458.3'421 C98-930779-4

Publisher: Nigel Berrisford

Editing: Paul Kropp Communications

Book design and layout: Karen Petherick, Markham, Ontario

Manufactured by Webcom Limited

Cover finish: Webcom's Exclusive DURACOAT

Contents

Getting Along in Italian

Benvenuti!

Welcome to *Getting Along In Italian*. This book is designed for quick and easy use for both the traveller and the beginning student of Italian. The material is organized according to topics you will need to see you through your visit. Every chapter begins with a general introduction and is followed by helpful phrases and essential vocabulary, as well as phrases you will hear in response to what you say.

Wherever possible, simple grammar is used to convey your message and questions.

When in doubt and ***When all else fails*** phrases are conveniently scattered throughout the book. These will help you out in many situations.

Simple English phonetics are used to achieve the sound of the spoken language. Bold face type will show you where to place the accent. Once you get a sense of the rhythm and sound of the language, you'll find Italian an easy and beautiful language to speak.

"BUON VIAGGIO!"
"HAVE A GOOD TRIP!"

Italian in a nutshell

Here's a list of the most basic expressions in Italian, well worth memorizing on your plane flight.

Hello!*/Goodbye.	Ciao! (Informal)	chow
Good morning (day).*	Buon giorno.	bwohn **johr**-noh
Good evening.*	Buona sera.	**bwoh**-nah **seh**-rah
Goodbye.	Arrivederci (ciao).	ahr-ree-veh-**dehr**-chee(chow)
Yes/No.	Sì / No.	see /noh
Okay.	Va bene.	vah **beh**-neh
Please.	Per piacere.	pehr pyah-**cheh**-reh
Thank you (very much).	(Mille) grazie.	(meel-leh) **grah**-tsyeh
You're welcome.	Prego.	**preh**-goh
Excuse me.	Mi scusi.	mee **skoo**-see
I'm Canadian.	Sono canadese.	**soh**-noh kah-nah-**deh**-zeh
Do you speak English?	Parla inglese?	**pahr**-lah een-**gleh**-zeh
I don't speak Italian.	Non parlo italiano.	nohn **pahr**-loh ee-tah-**lyah**-noh
I don't (didn't) understand.	Non capisco. (Non ho capito.)	nohn kah-**pee**-skoh (nohn oh kah-**pee**-toh)
What is this in Italian?	Come si dice questo in italiano?	**koh**-meh see **dee**-cheh **kweh**-stoh een ee-tah-**lyah**-noh
My name is...	Mi chiamo...	mee **kyah**-moh
Where is...?	Dov'è...?	dohv-**eh**
Please...	Per favore,... (just point if you don't know the word)	pehr fah-**voh**-reh

Ciao is very informal and is used most frequently between friends and acquaintances. It means hello, hi, bye, see you later. **Buon giorno** is used throughout the day until late afternoon. **Buona sera** is the standard greeting for the remainder of the day.

CHAPTER ONE

A pronunciation guide

Pronouncing vowels properly in Italian is the key to sounding like a native speaker. Simple English phonetics are used throughout the book to help you. Bearing in mind the rules below, you will soon be reading the Italian words directly, with perhaps only quick glances at the English phonetics if your listener looks puzzled.

PRONOUNCE EVERY LETTER

In Italian, every letter is usually pronounced. **Mio** is pronounced **mee**-oh. However, some vowels seem to share a syllable. **Ciao** is pronounced Chow and **piano** is pronounced **pyah**-noh.

Italian words are usually, but not always, stressed on the second-last syllable of the word. Exceptions are some foreign words and those that end in è or à: città (chee-**tah**), università (oo-nee-vehr-see-**tah**), caffè (kah-**feh**). If you are not sure, quickly glance at the English phonetic pronunciation. The stressed syllable will appear in **bold-face**.

Plurals are formed by changing the last letter of the noun. A noun ending in **a** changes to **e** (pizz**a** becomes pizz**e**). A noun ending in **o** changes to ***i*** (cappuccin**o** becomes cappuccin**i**). A noun ending in **e** changes to **i** (dolc**e** becomes dolc**i**). Foreign words and words like caffè and università that end in **è** and **à** do not change their endings.

ITALIAN LETTER	ENGLISH PHONETICS	ENGLISH SOUND AS IN...	ITALIAN YOU MAY KNOW
a	**ah**	father, yacht	piano (**pyah**-noh)
è	**eh**	exit, bet	dov'**è** (dohv-**eh**- where is...?)
e	**eh**	let	espresso *(eh-**sprehs**-soh)
i	**ee**	need, beet	vino (**vee**-noh)
o	**oh**	hope, cost	italiano (ee-tah-**lyah**-noh)
u	**oo**	cool, too	cappuccino (kahp-poo-**chee**-noh)
c followed by **i, e, è**	**ch**	cheese	ciao (chow)
c followed by **a, o, h**	**k**	coke	coca (**koh**-kah)
g followed by **i, e, è**	**j**	gentle gelato	gentile (jehn-**tee**-leh) (jeh-**lah**-toh)
g followed by **a, o, h**	**gh**	get	spaghetti (spah-**gheht**-tee)
gli - g is silent	**l**	million	bottiglia (boht-**tee**-lyah)
gn - g is silent	**ny**	canyon	lasagna (lah-**sah**-nyah)
qu	**kw**	quiet	questo (**kweh**-stoh)
sc - followed by i, e, u	**sh**	push	sci (shee - "skis")
z, zz	**ts, dz**	hits, kids	grazie (**grah**-tsyeh) zero (**dzeh**-roh)
r	trilled		Brrravo! (**Brrrah**-voh)

CHAPTER TWO

The basics

The following expressions have been grouped together for quick reference. You will use these over and over again in polite conversation and in many situations. Familiarize yourself with these and practice them out loud.

GREETINGS

Hello!*/Goodbye.	Ciao! (informal)	chow
Good morning (day).*	Buon giorno.	bwohn **johr**-noh
Good afternoon.*	(Buon pomeriggio.)	bwohn poh-mehr-**ree**-jyoh
Good evening.*	Buona sera.	**bwoh**-nah **seh**-rah
Good night.*	Buona notte.	**bwoh**-nah **noht**-teh
Goodbye.	Arrivederci (ciao).	ahr-ree-veh-**dehr**-chee
See you later.	A più tardi (ciao).	ah pyoo **tahr**-dee (chow)
See you soon.	A presto.	ah **preh**-stoh
Until tomorrow.	A domani.	ah doh-**mah**-nee
Let's go!	Andiamo!	ahn-**dyah**-moh

Buon giorno is used throughout the day until late afternoon. **Buona sera** is the standard greeting for the remainder of the day. **Buon pomeriggio** is rarely heard, except on radio and television broadcasts. **Buona notte** is used at the end of the evening, when leaving. **Ciao** is used most frequently and means hello, hi, bye, see you later.

INTRODUCTIONS & COURTESIES

My name is...	Mi chiamo...	mee **kyah**-moh
What's your name?	Lei, come si chiama?	lay, **koh**-meh see kyah-mah
How do you do?	Come sta?	**koh**-meh stah
How are you?	Come va?	**koh**-meh vah
Very well, thank you. And you?	Molto bene grazie. E lei?	**mohl**-toh **beh**-neh **grah**-tsyeh. eh lay
Pleased to meet you.	Molto piacere (lieto (-a)).	**mohl**-toh pyah-**cheh**-reh (**lyeh**-toh (-tah))
Okay/Sure.	D'accordo.	dahk-**kohr**-doh
Of course.	Certamente.	chehr-tah-**mehn**-teh
Perhaps.	Forse.	**fohr**-seh
Please.	Per piacere.	pehr pyah-**cheh**-reh
Thank you (very much).	(Mille) grazie.	(**meel**-leh) **grah**-tsyeh
You're welcome.	Prego.	**preh**-goh
Excuse me.	Mi scusi.	mee **skoo**-see
Excuse me (may I get through).	Permesso.	pehr-**mehs**-soh
I'm sorry.	Mi dispiace.	mee dees-**pyah**-cheh
No, thank you.	No, grazie.	noh **grah**-tsyeh
Just a second.	Un momento.	oon moh-**mehn**-toh
That's all right/Okay.	Va bene.	vah **beh**-neh
It doesn't matter.	Non importa/Di niente.	nohn eem-**pohr**-tah/ dee **nyehn**-teh
It's not a problem.	Non c'è problema.	nohn cheh proh-**bleh**-mah
I'm Canadian.	Sono canadese.	**soh**-noh kah-nah-**deh**-zeh
Do you speak English?	Parla inglese?	**pahr**-lah een-**gleh**-zeh
I don't speak Italian.	Non parlo italiano.	nohn **pahr**-loh ee-tah-**lyah**-noh
I speak a little Italian.	Parlo poco italiano.	**pahr**-loh poh-koh ee-tah-**lyah**-noh
I don't understand.	Non capisco/ Non ho capito.	nohn kah-**pee**-skoh/ nohn oh kah-**pee**-toh

What did you say?	Che cosa ha detto?	keh **koh**-zah ah **deht**-toh
Please speak slowly.	Per piacere, parli lentamente.	pehr pyah-**cheh**-reh, **pahr**-lee lehn-tah-**mehn**-teh
Please repeat (that).	Lo ripeta per favore.	loh ree-**peh**-tah pehr fah-**voh**-reh
Write it, please.	Lo scriv.	loh **skree**-vah
May I ask a question?	Posso fare una domanda?	**poh**-soh **fah**-reh **oo**-nah doh-**mahn**-dah
How do you say it in Italian?	Come si dice questo in italiano?	**koh**-meh see **dee**-cheh **kweh**-stoh een ee-tah-**lyah**-noh

DIRECTIONS

Could you please help me?	Può aiutarmi, per favore?	**pwoh** ah-yoo-**tahr**-mee pehr fah-**voh**-reh
I'm lost.	Non so dove mi trovo.	nohn soh **doh**-veh mee **troh**-voh
Which way do I go?...	*In che direzione devo andare?...*	*een keh dee-reh-**tsyoh**-neh **deh**-voh ahn-**dah**-reh*
left	a sinistra	ah see-**nee**-strah
right	a destra	ah **dehs**-trah
straight ahead	sempre diritto	**sehm**-preh dee-**reet**-toh
go back	in dietro	een **dyeh**-troh
Where are the toilets?	Dove si trova il gabinetto (bagno, toilette)?	**doh**-veh see **troh**-vah eel gah-bee-**neht**-toh (**bah**-nyoh, toh-eh-**leht**)
Men's bathroom	Signori/Uomini	see-**nyoh**-ree/ **woh**-mee-nee
Women's bathroom	Signore/Donne	see-**nyoh**-reh/**dohn**-neh
Where is the Canadian Embassy?	Dov'è l'ambasciata canadese (americana)?	dohv-**eh** lahm-bah-**shyah**-tah kah-nah-**deh**-seh (ah-meh-ree-**kah**-nah)

CHAPTER THREE

On your arrival

Passing through Italian Customs and Passport Control is very simple if all your papers and passports are up-to-date. Upon entering the country (or aboard your flight), you will be asked to fill out an **Identity Card**. Fill this out and hand it to the customs' officer along with your passport (and visa, if required).

SIGN LANGUAGE

AIRPORT TERMINAL	AEROPORTO	ah-eh-roh-**pohr**-toh
FASTEN YOUR SEAT BELTS	ALLACCIARE LE CINTURE DI SICUREZZA	ahl-lah-**chyah**-reh leh **cheen**-too-reh dee see-koo-**reht**-tsah
ARRIVALS	ARRIVI	ahr-**ree**-vee
BAGGAGE CLAIM	BAGAGLI	bah-**gah**-lyee
CONNECTIONS	COINCIDENZE	koh-een-chee-**dehn**-zeh
BAGGAGE CLAIM	DEPOSITO BAGAGLI (LEFT LUGGAGE)	deh-**poh**-see-toh bah-**gah**-lyee
NATIONAL AIRLINES	LINEE NAZIONALI	**lee**-neh-eh nah-tsyoh-**nah**-lee
INTERNATIONAL AIRLINES	LINEE INTERNAZIONALI	**lee**-neh-eh een-tehr-nah-tsyoh-**nah**-lee
DEPARTURES	PARTENZE	pahr-**tehn**-zeh

SIGN LANGUAGE

DANGER!	PERICOLO!	Peh-**ree**-koh-loh
BOARDING GATE	SALA D'IMBARCO	**sah**-lah deem-**bahr**-koh
WOMEN'S (TOILET)	SIGNORE, DONNE	see-**nyoh**-reh, **dohn**-neh
MEN'S (TOILET)	SIGNORI, UOMINI	see-**nyoh**-ree, **woh**-mee-nee
DRINKABLE/NON-DRINKABLE WATER	ACQUA (NON) POTABILE	**ah**-kwah (nohn) poh-**tah**-bee-leh
EXIT	USCITA	oo-**shee**-tah
NO EXIT	VIETATO USCIRE	vyeh-**tah**-toh oo-**shee**-reh
NO ENTRANCE	VIETATO ENTRARE	vyeh-**tah**-toh ehn-**tra**-reh
NO SMOKING	VIETATO FUMARE	vyeh-**tah**-toh foo-**mah**-reh
INTERNATIONAL FLIGHTS	VOLI INTERNAZIONALI	**voh**-lee een-tehr-nah-tsyoh-**nah**-lee
DOMESTIC FLIGHTS	VOLI NAZIONALI	**voh**-lee nah-tsyoh-**nah**-lee

CUSTOMS - LA DOGANA

Most visitors pass through with nothing to declare, carrying personal goods only. Check with your travel agent about what may be brought into Italy duty-free. In the unlikely event that you have goods to declare or are asked to go through an inspection...

What you may hear

Il passaporto, per favore.	Your passport, please.
Ha qualcosa da dichiarare?	Do you have anything to declare?
Può aprire la valigia, per cortesia?	Please, open your suitcase(s).
Deve pagare la dogana.	You'll have to pay duty on this.
Il controllo è finito.	The inspection is over.

Once through customs, you will see two signs:

MERCI da DICHIARARE	**GOODS TO DECLARE**
NULLA da DICHIARARE	**NOTHING TO DECLARE**

Things you might need to say

Where is...?	*Dov'è...?*	***doh**-veh*
customs	la dogana	lah doh-**gah**-nah
baggage claim	il deposito bagagli	eel deh-**poh**-see-toh bah-**gah**-lyee
Here (is)...	*Ecco...*	***ehk**-koh*
my passport	il mio passaporto	eel **mee**-oh pahs-sah-**pohr**-toh
my identity card	la mia carta d'identità	lah **mee**-ah **kahr**-tah dee-dehn-tee-**tah**
driver's license (international)	la mia patente (internazionale)	lah **mee**-ah pah-**tehn**-teh (een-tehr-nah-styoh-**nah**-leh)
my luggage	le mie valigie	leh **mee**-eh vah-**lee**-jyeh
I have nothing to declare.	Non ho niente (nulla) da dichiarare.	Nohn oh **nyehn**-teh (**nool**-lah) dah dee-kyah-**rah**-reh
I'm here on holidays.	Sono in vacanza.	**soh**-noh een vah-**kahn**-zeh
I'm here on business.	Sono in viaggio d'affari.	**soh**-noh een **vyahj**-joh dahf-**fah**-ree
I'll be staying...	*Resterò qui...*	*reh-steh-**roh** kwee*
a week	una settimana	**oon**-nah seht-tee-**mah**-nah
(10) days	dieci giorni	**dyeh**-chee **jyohr**-nee
a month	un mese	oon **meh**-zeh
I'm just passing through.	Sono solo di passaggio.	**soh**-noh **soh**-loh dee pahs-**sahj**-jyoh

BAGGAGE CLAIM

Where is tourist information?	Dov'è l'ufficio informazioni?	doh-**veh** loof-**fee**-chyoh een-fohr-mah-**tsyoh**-nee
Is this yours?	È vostra?	eh **voh**-strah
Yes, thank you, it's mine.	Si, grazie, questa è mia.	see, **grah**-tsyeh, **kweh**-stah eh **mee**-ah

Are there any luggage carts?	Dove si trova un carrello (portabagagli)?	**doh**-veh see **troh**-vah oon kahr-**rehl**-loh (pohr-tah-bah-**gah**-lyee)?
I need a porter.	Ho bisogno di un portabagagli.	oh bee-**zoh**-nyoh dee oon pohr-tah-bah-**gah**-lyee.
How much do I owe you?	Quanto le devo/ Quant'è?	**kwahn**-toh leh **deh**-voh?
I have lost my suitcase.	Mi manca una valigia.	mee **mahn**-kah **oo**-nah vah-**lee**-jyah
I have lost my luggage.	Mi mancano i miei bagagli.	mee **mahn**-cah-no ee mee-**ay** bah-**gah**-lyee
Where do I report it?	Dov'è l'ufficio oggetti smarriti?	doh-**veh** loof-**fee**-chyoh ohj-**jeht**-tee smah-**ree**-tee

MONEY

The best rate of exchange is usually at a National Bank, but banks close at 1:00 p.m. At cash exchange offices, always check the exchange rates and commissions charged to be sure you are getting a fair rate. Ask for a receipt and count your money before you leave the counter.

Where is the exchange desk?	Dov'è l'ufficio di cambio (la banca)?	**doh**-veh loof-**fee**-chyoh dee **kahm**-byoh (lah **bahn**-kah)
I want to change...	*Vorrei cambiare...*	*vohr-**ray** kahm-**byah**-reh*
$100	cento dollari	**chehn**-toh **dohl**-lah-ree
traveller's cheques	assegni da viaggiatori	ahs-**seh**-nyee dah vyahj-jah-**toh**-ree
When is the bank open/ closed?	A che ora aprono/ chiudono la banca?	ah keh **oh**-rah **ah**-proh-noh/**kyoo**-doh-noh lah **bahn**-kah
What is the rate?	Qual'è il cambio corrente?	kwahl-**eh** eel **kahm**-byoh kohr-**rehn**-teh
What commission do you charge?	Quale percentuale vi fate pagare?	**kwah**-leh pehr-chehn-**twah**-leh vee **fah**-teh pah-**gah**-reh

I'd like the money in...	*Vorrei i soldi...*	*vohr-**ray** ee **sohl**-dee*
big bills	in grosse banconote	een **grohs**-seh bahn-kah-**noh**-teh
small bills	in piccole banconote	een **peek**-koh-lee bahn-kah-**noh**-teh
in small change	in spiccioli.	een **spee**-choh-lee
Do you accept credit cards?	Si accettano carte di credito?	see ah-**cheh**-tah-noh **kahr**-teh dee **kreh**-dee-toh?

BUSES & TAXIS TO THE CITY

What bus (should I take)?	Quali autobus vanno in città?	**kwah**-lee **ow**-toh-boos **vahn**-noh een cheet-**tah**
How much is the fare?	Quant'è il biglietto?	kwahnt-**eh** eel bee-**lyeht**-toh
Where is the bus stop?	Dov'è la fermata dell'autobus?	dohv-**eh** lah fehr-**mah**-tah
Where can I get a taxi?	Dove posso prendere un taxi?	**doh**-veh **pohs**-soh **prehn**-deh-reh oon tahk-**see**
I would like to go to Hotel...	Vorrei andare all'Hotel...	vohr-**ray** ahn-**dah**-reh ahl-**oh**-tehl
How much?	Quanto costa?	**kwahn**-toh **koh**-stah
Are you free?	È libero?	eh **lee**-beh-roh
Here's the address.	Ecco l'indirizzo.	**ehk**-koh leen-dee-**ree**-tsoh
Keep the change.	Tenga il resto.	**tehn**-gah eel **reh**-stoh
Thank you. Goodbye.	Grazie. Arrivederci.	**grah**-tsyeh. ahr-ree-veh-**dehr**-chee

What you may hear

Si. È libero.	see. eh **lee**-beh-roh	Yes. I'm free.
Dove andate?	**doh**-veh ahn-**dah**-teh	Where do you want to go?
È diecimila lire.	eh dyeh-chee-**mee**-lah **lee**-reh	You owe (10000 lire).

HANDY TAXI PHRASES

Do you know where it is?	Sa dove si trova?	sah **doh**-veh see **troh**-vah
Is there an extra fee?	C'è un sovrapprezzo?	cheh oon soh-vrah-**preh**-tsoh
I'll pay only what's on the meter.	Pago solo la cifra sul tassametro.	**pah**-goh **soh**-loh lah **chee**-frah sool tahs-sah-**meh**-troh
I'm in a hurry.	Ho fretta.	oh **freht**-tah
Hurry!	Più veloce (presto)!	pyoo veh-**loh**-cheh (**preh**-stoh)
Slow down!	Più piano, per cortesia!	pyoo **pyah**-noh, pehr kohr-teh-**zee**-ah
Stop here (at the corner)!	Si fermi qui (all'angolo)!	see **fehr**-mee kwee (ahl-**ahn**-goh-loh)
Stop at the next street.	Si fermi alla prossima via.	see **fehr**-mee **ahl**-lah **prohs**-see-mah **vee**-ah
Wait (for me).	Mi aspetti.	mee ah-**speht**-tee
Wait a minute.	Un momento.	Oon moh-**mehn**-toh
	Torno subito.	**tohr**-noh **soo**-bee-toh
I can't change that bill.	Non ho da cambiare.	nohn oh dah kahm-**byah**-reh

When you get to your hotel, use a little care before washing your hands, In Italian, **F** stands for **freddo** (cold water) and **C** stands for **caldo** - take care that you don't mistake the **C** for the cold water tap!

Il gabinetto, **toilette**, **W.C.** are all names for public washrooms. **Il bagno** refers to a toilet in someone's residence.

CHAPTER FOUR

Telling time and making appointments

In answer to "What time is it?", "**Che ora è?**" (Keh **oh**-rah eh?), you will usually be told or shown a clock. However, if you need to make an appointment or a time to meet later, you will need to know some basic phrases and vocabulary.

What time is it?	*Che ora è?*	*keh **oh**-rah eh*
It is...	*È...*	*eh*
noon	mezzogiorno	mehd-dzoh-**jyohr**-noh
1:00	l'una	**loo**-nah
midnight	mezzanotte	meh-dzah-**noht**-teh
early/late	presto/tardi	**preh**-stoh/**tahr**-dee
It is...	*Sono...*	***soh**-noh...*
2:00, 3:00, 4:00	le due, le tre, le quattro	leh **doo**-eh, leh tre, le **kwah**-troh
5:15 (a quarter past)	le cinque e un quarto	leh **cheen**-kweh eh oon **kwahr**-toh
9:05	le nove e cinque	leh **noh**-veh eh **cheen**-kweh
10:30 (half past)	le dieci e mezzo	leh **dyeh**-chee eh **mehd**-dzoh
7:40	le sette meno venti	leh **seht**-teh **meh**-noh **vehn**-tee
a.m.	del mattino	dehl maht-**tee**-noh
in the afternoon	del pomeriggio	dehl poh-meh-**ree**-jyoh
p.m.	della notte	**dehl**-lah **noht**-teh

> Remember train, plane, boat, transit schedules, as well as office and shop hours, are on the 24-hour clock.

APPOINTMENTS

When are we meeting?	Quando ci vediamo?	**kwahn**-doh chee veh-**dyah**-moh
today	oggi	**ohj**-jee
tomorrow	domani	doh-**mah**-nee
the day after tomorrow	dopodomani	doh-poh-doh-**mah**-nee
yesterday	ieri	ee-**yeh**-ree
in the morning	nella mattina	**nehl**-lah maht-**tee**-nah
in the afternoon	nel pomeriggio	nehl poh-meh-**ree**-jyoh
in the evening	di sera	dee **seh**-rah
tonight	stasera	stah-**seh**-rah

DAYS OF THE WEEK

Today (is)...	*Oggi è...*	***ohj**-jee eh*
Monday	lunedì	**loo**-neh-dee
Tuesday	martedì	**mahr**-teh-dee
Wednesday	mercoledì	mehr-**koh**-leh-dee
Thursday	giovedì	**jyoh**-veh-dee
Friday	venerdì	**veh**-nehr-dee
Saturday	sabato	**sah**-bah-toh
Sunday	domenica	doh-**meh**-nee-kah

MONTHS

January	gennaio	jehn-**nah**-yoh
February	febbraio	fehb-**brah**-yoh
March	marzo	**mahr**-tzoh
April	aprile	ah-**pree**-leh
May	maggio	**mah**-jyoh

MONTHS

June	giugno	**joo**-nyoh
July	luglio	**loo**-lyoh
August	agosto	ah-**goh**-stoh
September	settembre	seht-**tehm**-breh
October	ottobre	oht-**toh**-breh
November	novembre	noh-**vehm**-breh
December	dicembre	dee-**chehm**-breh

PUBLIC HOLIDAYS

January 1	CAPODANNO	NEW YEAR'S DAY
Easter Monday	LUNEDI DOPO PASQUA	EASTER MONDAY
April 25	FESTA DELLA RESISTENZA	LIBERATION DAY (1945)
May 1	FESTA DEL LAVORO	LABOR DAY
June 2	FESTA DELLA REPUBBLICA	PROCLAMATION OF REPUBLIC
August 15	ASSUNZIONE (FERRAGOSTO)	ASSUMPTION DAY
November 1	OGNISSANTI	ALL SAINTS' DAY
December 8	IMMACOLATA CONCEZIONE	IMMACULATE CONCEPTION
December 25	NATALE	CHRISTMAS

SEASON'S GREETINGS & BEST WISHES!

Happy Holidays!	Buone Feste!	**bwoh**-neh **feh**-steh
Merry Christmas!	Buon Natale!	bwohn nah-**tah**-leh
Happy New Year!	Buon Anno!	bwohn **ahn**-noh
Congratulations!	Congratulazioni!	kohn-grah-too-lah-**tsyoh**-nee
Good luck!	Buona fortuna!	**bwoh**-nah fohr-**too**-nah
All the best!	Auguri!	ow-**goo**-ree
Happy Name Day!	Buon onomastico!	bwohn oh-noh-**mah**-stee-koh
Happy Birthday!	Buon compleanno!	bwohn kom-pleh-**ahn**-noh
Have a good trip!	Buon viaggio!	bwohn vee-ah-**jyoh**

NUMBERS

0	zero	**dzeh**-roh
1	uno	**oo**-noh
2	due	**doo**-eh
3	tre	treh
4	quattro	**kwaht**-troh
5	cinque	**cheen**-kweh
6	sei	**seh**-ee
7	sette	**seht**-teh
8	otto	**oht**-toh
9	nove	**noh**-veh
10	dieci	**dyeh**-chee
11	undici	**oon**-dee-chee
12	dodici	**doh**-dee-chee
13	tredici	**treh**-dee-chee
14	quattordici	kwah-**tohr**-dee-chee
15	quindici	**kween**-dee-chee
16	sedici	**seh**-dee-chee
17	diciassette	dee-chyah-**seht**-teh
18	diciotto	dee-**chyoht**-toh
19	diciannove	dee-chyah-**noh**-veh
20	venti	**vehn**-tee
21	ventuno	vehnt-**oo**-noh
22	ventidue	vehn-tee-**doo**-eh
23, etc.	ventitrè, ecc.	vehn-tee-**treh**
30	trenta	**trehn**-tah
40	quaranta	kwah-**rahn**-tah
50	cinquanta	cheen-**kwahn**-tah
60	sessanta	sehs-**sahn**-tah
70	settanta	seht-**tahn**-tah
80	ottanta	oht-**tahn**-tah
90	novanta	noh-**vahn**-tah
100	cento	**chehn**-toh
101	centuno	chehnt-**oo**-noh
102	centodue	chehn-toh-**doo**-eh
150, etc.	centocinquanta, ecc.	chehn-toh-cheen-**kwahn**-tah

200	duecento	doo-eh-**chehn**-toh
300	trecento	treh-**chehn**-toh
400	quattrocento	kwaht-troh-**chehn**-toh
500	cinquecento	cheen-kweh-**chehn**-toh
600	seicento	say-**chehn**-toh
700	settecento	seht-teh-**chehn**-toh
800	ottocento	oht-toh-**chehn**-toh
900	novecento	noh-veh-**chehn**-toh
1,000	mille	**meel**-leh
1,500	millecinquecento	meel-leh-cheen-kweh-**chehn**-toh
2,000, 3,000, etc.	duemila, tremila, ecc.	doo-eh-**mee**-lah, treh-**mee**-lah
10,000	diecimila	dyeh-chee-**mee**-lah
50,000	cinquantamila	cheen-kwahn-tah-**mee**-lah
100,000	centomila	chehn-toh-**mee**-lah
200,000	duecentomila	doo-eh-chehn-toh-**mee**-lah
1,000,000	un milione	oon mee-**lyoh**-neh
2,000,000	due milioni	doo-eh mee-**lyoh**-nee
1,000,000,000	un miliardo	oon mee-**lyahr**-doh

Ordinal Numbers

1st	primo	**pree**-moh
2nd	secondo	seh-**kohn**-doh
3rd	terzo	**tehr**-tsoh
4th	quarto	**kwahr**-toh
5th	quinto	**kween**-toh
6th	sesto	**sehs**-toh
7th	settimo	**seht**-tee-moh
8th	ottavo	oht-**tah**-voh
9th	nono	**noh**-noh
10th	decimo	**deh**-chee-moh
11th	undicesimo	oon-dee-**cheh**-zee-moh
12th	dodicesimo	doh-dee-**cheh**-zee-moh
100th	centesimo	chehn-**teh**-zee-moh
1,000th	millesimo	meel-**leh**-zee-moh

CHAPTER FIVE

Getting acquainted

Italians greet each other warmly, using Buon giorno (bwon **johr**-noh), Ciao! (Chow!), Come va? (**Koh**-meh vah?), or Come stai? (**Koh**-meh **stah**-ee?). Friends shake hands, hug or kiss each other on each cheek or a combination of all three. Some form of touch usually accompanies meetings and greetings, even between men.

GREETINGS, AGAIN

Good morning.	Buon giorno.	bwon **johr**-noh
Good evening.	Buona sera.	**bwoh**-nah **seh**-rah
Good night.	Buona notte.	**bwoh**-nah **noht**-teh
Hello/Goodbye.	Ciao!.	chow
See you soon.	A presto.	ah **prehs**-toh
See you later.	A più tardi (Ciao).	ah pyoo **tahr**-dee (chow)
See you tomorrow.	A domani.	ah doh-**mah**-nee
Let's go.	Andiamo.	ahn-**dyah**-moh
Goodbye.	Arrivederci.	ah-ree-veh-**dehr**-chee
Do you speak English?	Parla inglese?	**pahr**-lah een-**gleh**-zeh
Yes/No.	Sì/No.	see/noh

signore, signora, signorina are not capitalized, except when addressing letters. Use **signora** only when you are absolutely sure of a lady's marital status, otherwise use **signorina**.

I'm a tourist.	Sono turista.	**soh**-noh too-**ree**-stah
I don't speak Italian.	Non parlo italiano.	nohn **pahr**-loh ee-tah-**lyah**-noh
I speak very little.	Parlo poco l'italiano.	**pahr**-loh **poh**-koh
I understand a little.	Capisco un pò.	kah-**pee**-skoh oon **poh**
Please, speak more slowly.	Per favore, parli più adagio.	pehr fah-**voh**-reh **pahr**-lee pyoo ah-**dah**-jyoh
Please repeat (that).	Lo ripeta per favore.	loh ree-**peh**-tah pehr fah-**voh**-reh
I understand (understood).	Capisco (ho capito).	kah-**pee**-skoh (oh kah-**pee**-toh)
I don't (didn't) understand.	Non capisco (non ho capito).	nohn kah-**pee**-skoh (nohn oh kah-**pee**-toh)

QUESTIONS & QUESTION WORDS

Who?	Chi?	kee
What?	Che cosa?	keh **koh**-zah
Why?	Perché?	pehr-**keh**
When?	Quando?	**kwahn**-doh
Where?	Dove?	**doh**-veh
How?	Come?	**koh**-meh
How much?	Quanto?	**kwahn**-toh
May I ask a question?	Posso fare una domanda?	**pohs**-soh **fah**-reh **oo**-nah doh-**mahn**-dah
Could you please help me?	Può aiutarmi, per favore?	**pwoh** ah-yoo-**tahr**-mee, pehr fah-**voh**-reh
Okay/Sure.	D'accordo.	dahk-**kohr**-doh
Of course.	Certamente.	chehr-tah-**mehn**-teh
What does that mean?	Che cosa significa (quello)?	keh **koh**-zah **seeg**-nyee-fee-kah **kwehl**-loh
What do you call this (that) in Italian?	Come si chiama questo (quello) in italiano?	**koh**-meh see **kyah**-mah **kwehs**-toh (**kwehl**-loh) een ee-tah-**lyah**-noh
Where is the (public) toilette?	Dov'è il toilette?	dohv-**eh** eel toh-eh-**leht**

INTRODUCTIONS

I'd like to introduce you to...	*Vorrei presentarLe...*	***vohr**-ray preh-sehn-**tahr**-leh*
Mr. Alessandro Rossi	il signor Alessandro Rossi	eel see-**nyohr** ah-lehs-**sahn**-droh **rohs**-see
Mrs. Elena Rossi	la signora Elena Rossi	lah see-**nyoh**-rah **eh**-leh-nah **rohs**-see
Miss/Ms Natalie Rossi	la signorina Natalie Rossi	lah see-nyoh-**ree**-nah **nah**-tah-lee **rohs**-see

Italian sentences are easy to form using **È**... (This is...) or **Ecco**...(Here is (are)...) by adding the words listed below in the ***MINI DICTIONARY***.

This is (my)...	**È**...	eh...
Here is (are) (my)...	**Ecco**...	**ehk**-koh...

**my is optional and the correct form is provided.

FAMILY & FRIENDS

MINI-DICTIONARY

aunt	mia zia	**mee**-ah **dzee**-yah
brother	mio fratello	**mee**-oh frah-**tehl**-loh
brother-in-law	mio cognato	**mee**-oh koh-**nyah**-toh
colleague (male)	il mio collega	eel **mee**-oh kohl-**leh**-gah
colleague (female)	la mia collega	lah **mee**-ah kohl-**leh**-gah
cousin (male)	mio cugino	**mee**-oh koo-**jee**-noh
cousin (female)	mia cugina	**mee**-ah koo-**jee**-nah
daughter	mia figlia	**mee**-ah **fee**-lyah
father-in-law	mio suocero	**mee**-oh **swoh**-cheh-roh
dad (father)	mio padre (papa)	**mee**-oh **pah**-dreh (pah-**pah**)
friend (male)	il mio amico	(eel) **mee**-oh ah-**mee**-koh
friend (female)	la mia amica	(lah) **mee**-ah ah-**mee**-kah
grandfather	mio nonno	**mee**-oh **nohn**-noh
grandmother	mia nonna	mee-ah **nohn**-nah

husband	mio marito	**mee**-oh mah-**ree**-toh
mother (mom)	mia madre (mamma)	**mee**-ah **mah**-dreh (**mahm**-mah)
mother-in-law	mia suocera	**mee**-ah **swoh**-cheh-rah
parents	(i) miei genitori	(ee) mee-yahy jeh-nee-**toh**-ree
sister	mia sorella	**mee**-ah soh-**rehl**-lah
sister-in-law	mia cognata	**mee**-ah koh-**nyah**-tah
son	mio figlio	**mee**-oh **fee**-lyoh
uncle	mio zio	**mee**-oh **dzee**-oh
wife	mia moglie	**mee**-ah **moh**-lyeh

In response to an introduction:

Pleased (to meet you)!	Molto lieto (lieta).	**mohl**-toh **lyeh**-toh(-tah)
Very pleased to meet you!	Molto piacere.	**mohl**-toh pyah-**cheh**-reh
A pleasure (the pleasure is mine).	Piacere mio.	pyah-**cheh**-reh **mee**-oh
How are you?	Come sta?	**koh**-meh **stah**
Fine, thanks. And you?	Bene, grazie. E lei?	**beh**-neh, **grah**-tsyeh eh lay
How's it going?	Come va?	**koh**-meh **vah**
Well, thank you.	Bene, grazie.	**beh**-neh, **grah**-tsyeh

PERSONAL INFORMATION

Where do you live?	*Dove abita?*	***doh**-veh **ah**-bee-tah*
I live in...	*Abito...*	***ah**-bee-toh*
Canada	in Canada	een kah-nah-**dah**
Toronto	a Toronto	ah toh-**rohn**-toh
How old are you?	*Quanti anni ha?*	***kwahn**-tee **ahn**-nee ah*
I (am)...(46).	Ho quaranta sei anni.	oh **kwah**-rahn-tah say **ahn**-nee
How old is he/she?	Quanti anni ha lui/lei?	**kwahn**-tee **ahn**-nee ah **loo**-ee/**lay**
He/she is...(52).	Ha cinquanta due anni.	ah chen-**kwahn**-tah **doo**-eh **ahn**-nee
Are you married?	È sposato (-a)?	eh spoh-**sah**-toh (-ah)
I (am)...married.	Sono sposato (-a).	**soh**-noh spoh-**sah**-toh (spoh-**sah**-tah)

I'm single.	No, sono celibe.	noh, **soh**-noh **cheh**-lee-beh
I'm a widower/widow.	Sono vedovo (-a).	**soh**-noh **veh**-doh-voh (**veh**-doh-vah)
Do you have any children?	Ha famiglia (figli)?	ah-fah-**mee**-lyah (**fee**-lyee)
How many?	*Quanti?*	***kwahn**-tee*
One daughter	Una figlia (due figlie). (two daughters).	**oo**-nah **fee**-lyah (**doo**-eh **fee**-lyee)
One son (two sons).	Un figlio (due figli).	oon **fee**-lyoh (**doo**-eh fee-lyee)
What is your occupation/ profession?	Che professione esercita?	keh proh-fehs-**syoh**-neh eh-**sehr**-chee-tah
What do you do?	Che cosa fa?	keh **koh**-zah fah
Where do you work?	Dove lavora?	**doh**-veh lah-**voh**-rah
I'm not working anymore.	Non lavoro più.	nohn lah-**voh**-roh pyoo
I'm retired.	Sono in pensione/ Sono pensionato (-a).	**soh**-noh een pehn-**syoh**-neh/**soh**-noh pehn-syoh-**nah**-toh(-ah)

MINI-DICTIONARY: OCCUPATIONS

I am...(a, an)...	*Sono...(un, una)...*	***soh**-noh (oon, **oon**-nah)*
accountant	(un) commercialista	kohm-mehr-chyah-**lee**-stah
architect	(un) architetto	ahr-kee-**teht**-toh
artist	(un) artista	ahr-**tee**-stah
baker	(un) fornaio	fohr-**nah**-yoh
businessman	(un) uomo d'affari	**woh**-moh dahf-**fah**-ree
butcher	(un) macellaio	mah-chehl-**lah**-yoh
carpenter	(un) falegname	fah-leh-**nyah**-meh
clerk	(un)(un') impiegato (-a)	eem-pyeh-**gah**-toh(-tah)
cook	(un)(una) cuoco (-a)	**kwoh**-koh(-kah)
dentist	(un) dentista	dehn-**tee**-stah
doctor	(un) dottore/ (una) dottoressa	doht-**toh**-reh/ doht-toh-**rehs**-sah
economist	(un) economista	eh-koh-noh-**mee**-stah
editor	(un) redattore	reh-daht-**toh**-reh

electrician	(un) elettricista	eh-leh-tree-**chee**-stah
engineer	(un) ingegnere	een-jehn-**nyeh**-reh
farmer	(un) agricoltore	ah-gree-kohl-**toh**-reh
film director	(un) direttore	dee-reht-**toh**-reh,
	(una) direttrice	dee-reht-**tree**-cheh
hairdresser	(un) parrucchiere	pahr-roo-**kyeh**-reh
journalist	(un) giornalista	jyohr-nah-**lee**-stah
lawyer	(un) avvocato	ahv-voh-**kah**-toh
manufacturer	(un) fabbricante,	fahb-bree-**kahn**-teh
	(un) industriale	een-doo-stree-**ah**-leh
mechanic	(un) meccanico	mehk-kah-**nee**-koh
musician	(un) musicista	moo-zee-**chee**-stah
nurse	(un') infermiera	een-fehr-**myeh**-rah
painter	(un) pittore/(una) pittrice	peet-**toh**-reh/pee-**tree**-chen
pilot	(un) pilotta	pee-**loht**-tah
professor	(un) professore/	proh-fehs-**soh**-reh/
	(una) professoressa	proh-fehs-soh-**rehs**-sah
salesperson	(un)(una) commesso (-a)	kohm-**mehs**-soh (-sah)
scientist	(uno) scienziato	shyehn-**tsyah**-toh
sculptor	(uno) scultore/	skool-**toh**-reh/
	(una) scultrice	skool-**tree**-cheh
shopkeeper	(un) negoziante	neh-goh-**tsyahn**-teh
student	(uno) studente/	stoo-**dehn**-teh/
	(una) studentessa	stoo-dehn-**tehs**-sah
teacher	(un)(una) maestro (-a)	mah-**eh**-stroh(-stah)
waiter, waitress	(un)(una) cameriere (-a)	kah-meh-**ryeh**-reh(-rah)
writer	(uno) scrittore/	skree-**toh**-reh/
	(una) scrittrice	skree-**tree**-cheh

SOCIALIZING

May I buy you...?	*Posso offrirLe...?*	***pohs**-soh ohf-**freer**-leh*
a drink	qualcosa da bere	kwahl-**koh**-zah dah **beh**-reh
a coffee	un caffè	oon kahf-**feh**
With pleasure!	Con piacere.	kohn pyah-**cheh**-reh

Gladly.	Volentieri.	voh-lehn-**tyeh**-ree
Cheers.	Salute.	sah-**loo**-teh
Do you mind if I smoke?	Le dispiace se fumo?	lay dee-**spyah**-cheh seh **foo**-moh
Not at all.	Per niente.	pehr **nyehn**-teh
Yes, it bothers me.	Si, mi dà fastidio.	see, mee dah fah-**stee**-dyoh
I'm married.	Sono sposato (-a).	**soh**-noh spoh-**zah**-toh (-tah)
I'm not married.	Non sono sposato (-a).	nohn **soh**-noh spoh-**zah**-toh (-tah)
I have a boyfriend/ girlfriend.	Ho il ragazzo/ la ragazza.	oh eel rah-**gah**-tsoh/ lah rah-**gah**-tsah
That's okay!	Non importa.	nohn eem-**pohr**-tah
Let's just be friends!	Solo amici.	**soh**-loh ah-**mee**-chee
Can I give you a ride?	Posso darLe un passaggio?	**pohs**-soh **dahr**-lee oon pahs-**sah**-jyoh
I'll take a taxi.	Prendo un taxi.	**prehn**-doh oon tahk-**see**
Can I see you again?	Ti posso rivedere?	tee **pohs**-soh ree-veh-**deh**-reh
Yes/No!	Si/ No!	see/noh
Thanks for everything.	Grazie di tutto.	**grah**-tsyeh dee **toot**-toh

Things You May Need To Say!

I'm travelling with a friend.	Viaggio con un amico (un' amica).	vee-**ah**-jyoh kohn oon ah-**mee**-koh (**oo**-nah ah-**mee**-kah)
We're leaving tomorrow.	Partiamo domani.	pahr-**tyah**-moh doh-**mah**-nee
Go away!	Se ne vada!	seh neh **vah**-dah
Leave me alone!	Mi lasci in pace!	mee **lah**-shee een **pah**-cheh
I'm going to call the police.	Adesso chiamo la polizia.	ah-**dehs**-soh **kyah**-moh lah poh-lee-**tsee**-yah

CHAPTER SIX

Accommodations

HOTELS

There are many types of hotels and residences converted to hotels throughout Italy. **Pensioni** (pehn-**syoh**-nee) are smaller dwellings converted into boarding houses. They are often homes typical of the region and may overlook a charming courtyard. They are less expensive than hotels and offer full or partial board. Hotels and most **Alberghi** (ahl-**behr**-ghee) are rated one to five stars or luxury class. Youth hostels, **Ostello** (oh-**stehl**-loh), offer low prices and a chance to meet students from around the world.

SIGN LANGUAGE

BANK	BANCA	**bahn**-kah
CAFÉ	CAFFÈ	kahf-**feh**
VACANCY	CAMERE LIBERE	**kah**-meh-reh **lee**-beh-reh
NO VACANCY	COMPLETO	kohm-**pleh**-toh
LUGGAGE CHECKROOM	DEPOSITO BAGAGLI	dee-**poh**-zee-toh bah-**gah**-lyee
MANAGER ON DUTY	DIRETTORE	dee-reht-**toh**-reh
NEWSSTAND	GIORNALI	jyohr-**nah**-lee
CURRENCY EXCHANGE DESK	IL CAMBIO	eel **kahm**-byoh
INFORMATION (HOTEL SERVICES)	INFORMAZIONI	een-fohr-mah-**tsyoh**-nee
REGISTRATION DESK	REGISTRAZIONE	reh-jee-strah-tsee-**oh**-neh
RESTAURANT	RISTORANTE	ree-stoh-**rahn**-teh

REGISTRATION

I have a reservation.	Ho prenotazione.	oh preh-noh-tah-**tsyoh**-neh
My name is...	Mi chiamo...	mee **kyah**-moh
My surname is...	Il mio cognome è...	eel **mee**-oh koh-**nyoh**-meh eh
Does this room have...?	*(Questa camera) ha...?*	*(**kweh**-stah **kah**-meh-rah) ah*
air conditioning	l'aria condizionata	**lah**-ree-ah kohn-dee-tsyoh-**nah**-tah
a double bed	il letto matrimoniale*	eel **leht**-toh mah-tree-moh-**nyah**-leh
two beds	due letti**	**doo**-eh **leht**-tee
a (private) bath	il bagno privato	eel **bah**-nyoh pree-**vah**-toh
hot water	l'acqua calda	**lahk**-kwah **kahl**-dah
a shower	la doccia	lah **doh**-chyah
a phone	il telefono	eel teh-**leh**-foh-noh
a television	il televisore	eel teh-leh-vee-**soh**-reh
What floor is it on?	A che piano è?	ah keh **pyah**-noh eh?
Is there an elevator?	C'è l'ascensore?	cheh lah-shehn-**soh**-reh?
May I see this room?	Potrei vedere la camera?	poh-tray veh-**deh**-reh lah **kah**-meh-rah?
I would like a...	*Vorrei una camera...*	*vohr-**ray** **oo**-nah **kah**-meh-rah*
bigger room	più grande	pyoo **grahn**-deh
smaller room	più piccola	pyoo **peek**-koh-lah
better room	di meglio	dee **meh**-lyoh
cheaper room	meno costosa	**meh**-noh koh-**stoh**-zah
quieter room	più quieta	pyoo kwee-**eh**-tah
Here is my passport.	Ecco il mio passaporto.	**ehk**-koh eel **mee**-oh pahs-sah-**pohr**-toh
What time is check-out?	A che ora devo lasciare la camera?	ah keh **oh**-rah **deh**-voh lah-**shah**-reh lah **kah**-meh-rah?

If you want a room for two with a double bed, ask for **una camera matrimoniale,** otherwise you may end up with two single beds - **una camera con due letti!**

BOOKING A ROOM

I don't have a reservation.	Non ho prenotazione.	nohn oh preh-noh-tah-**tsyoh**-neh
I would like a room for tonight.	Vorrei una camera per stanotte.	vohr-**ray** oo-nah **kah**-meh-rah pehr stah-**noht**-teh
I need a...	*Vorrei una camera...*	*vohr-**ray** **oo**-nah **kah**-meh-rah*
single room	singola	**seen**-goh-lah
with a double bed	matrimoniale	mah-tree-moh-**nyah**-leh
double room (with two beds)	doppia	**dohp**-pyah
I need a room...	*Vorrei una camera...*	*vohr-**ray** **oo**-nah **kah**-meh-rah*
with private bath	con bagno privato	kohn **bah**-nyoh pree-**vah**-toh
with a shower	con doccia	kohn **doh**-chyah
a non-smoking room	ai non fumatori	**ah**-ee nohn foo-mah-**toh**-ree
with a balcony	con terrazzino	kohn teh-raht-**tsee**-noh
with a sea view	che dia sul mare	keh **dee**-ah sool **mah**-reh
facing (away from) the street	che (non) dia sulla strada	keh (nohn) **dee**-ah **sool**-lah **strah**-dah
facing the courtyard	che dia sul cortile	keh **dee**-ah sool kohr-**tee**-leh
How much does this room cost?	Quant'è la camera?	kwahnt-**eh** lah **kah**-meh-rah
May I see this room?	Potrei vedere la camera?	poh-**tray** veh-**deh**-reh lah **kah**-meh-rah
I don't like it.	Non mi piace.	nohn mee **pyah**-cheh

I'll take this room for...	*La prendo per...*	*lah **prehn**-doh pehr*
one night	una notte	**oo**-nah **noht**-teh
a few nights	alcune notti	ahl-**koo**-neh **noht**-tee
one week	una settimana	**oo**-nah seht-tee-**mah**-nah
How much...?	*Quanto si paga...?*	***kwahn**-toh see **pah**-gah*
with breakfast	con colazione	kohn koh-laht-**tsyoh**-neh
with the American plan	con pensione completa	kohn pehn-**syoh**-neh kohm-**pleht**-tah
without meals	senza i pasti	**sehn**-zah **pah**-stee
Is everything included?	È tutto compreso?	eh **toot**-toh kohm-**preh**-soh
How much do you charge for children?	Quanto fanno pagare per i bambini?	**kwahn**-toh **fahn**-noh pah-**gah**-reh pehr ee bahm-**bee**-nee

AT THE FRONT DESK

The key to my room (#318), please.	Per cortesia, la chiave per numero trecento diciotto.	pehr kohr-teh-**zee**-ah, lah **kyah**-vee peh **noo**-meh-roh treh-**chehn**-toh dee-**chyoht**-toh.
Are there any...for me?	*Ci sono...per me?*	*chee **soh**-noh...pehr meh*
messages	dei messaggi	**deh**-ee mehs-**sah**-jee
letters	delle lettere	**dehl**-leh **leh**-teh-reh
Did anyone call for me?	Mi ha cercato qualcuno?	mee ah chehr-**kah**-toh kwahl-**koo**-noh
My passport, please.	Il mio passaporto, per favore.	eel **mee**-oh pahs-sah-**pohr**-toh, perh fah-**voh**-reh
I'd like to speak to the manager.	Vorrei parlare con il direttore.	vohr-**ray** pahr-**lah**-reh kohn eel dee-reht-**toh**-reh
It's very important.	È molto importante.	eh **mohl**-toh eem-pohr-**tahn**-teh
Please call me at 6:00 a.m.	Per favore, mi chiama alle sei di mattina.	pehr fah-**voh**-reh, mee **kyah**-mah **ahl**-leh **seh**-ee dee maht-**tee**-nah

I need a translator.	Ho bisogno di un interprete.	oh bee-**zoh**-nyoh dee oon een-**tehr**-preh-teh

HOTEL SERVICES

Where is (the)....?	*Dov'è...?*	*doh-**veh***
barber's	il parrucchiere (barbiere)	eel pah-roo-**kyeh**-reh
hairdresser's	la parrucchiera	lah pah-rook-**kyeh**-rah
bank	la banca	la **bahn**-kah
café	il caffè	eel kah-**feh**
currency exchange desk	il cambio	eel **kahm**-byoh
information desk	gli informazioni	lee een-fohr-mah-**tsyoh**-nee
luggage checkroom	deposito bagagli	deh-**poh**-zee-toh bah-**gah**-lyee
manager	il direttore	eel dee-reh-**toh**-reh
Where is (the)....?	*Dov'è...?*	*doh-**veh***
post office - telegraph	la posta e telegrafi	lah **poh**-stah eh teh-leh-**grah**-fee
restaurant	il ristorante	eel ree-stoh-**rahn**-teh
toilet	i gabinetti (il toilette)	ee gah-bee-**neht**-tee (eel toh-eh-**leht**)

PERSONAL NEEDS

Please, bring me... (a, an)...	*Per piacere, mi manda...*	*pehr pyah-**cheh**-reh mee **mahn**-dah*
ashtray	un portacenere	oon pohr-tah-**cheh**-neh-reh
blanket	una coperta	oo-nah koh-**pehr**-tah
glass	un bicchiere	oon beek-**kyeh**-reh
(some) hangers	delle grucce	**dehl**-leh **groo**-cheh
pillow	un cuscino	oon koo-**shee**-noh
(a bar of) soap	una saponetta	oo-nah sah-poh-**neht**-tah
(some) toilet paper	della carta igienica	dehl-lah **kahr**-tah ee-**jeh**-nee-kah
towel	un asciugamano	oon ah-shoo-gah-**mah**-noh

This room needs to be cleaned.	Bisogna pulire questa camera.	bee-**zoh**-nyoh poo-**lee**-reh **kweh**-stah **kah**-meh-rah
When can you clean my room? (As soon as possible.)	Quando può farla pulire? (Il più presto possibile.)	**kwahn**-doh **pwoh fahr**-lah (eel pyoo **preh**-stoh pohs-**see**-bee-leh)

LAUNDRY

Can I have this...?	*Può farlo...?*	*pwoh **fahr**-loh*
dry-cleaned	lavare a secco	lah-**vah**-reh ah-**sehk**-koh
pressed only	solo stirare	**soh**-loh stee-**rah**-reh
repaired	rammendare	rahm-mehn-**dah**-reh
washed	lavare	lah-**vah**-reh
When will it be ready?	Quando sarà pronto?	**kwahn**-doh sah-**rah** **prohn**-toh
I need it...	*Ho bisogno...*	*oh bee-**zoh**-nyoh*
as soon as possible	il più presto possibile	eel pyoo **preh**-stoh pohs-**see**-bee-leh
today	oggi	**ohj**-jee
tomorrow	domani	doh-**mah**-nee
Please be careful (with this).	Per cortesia, stia attento.	pehr kohr-teh-**zee**-ah, **stee**-ah aht-**tehn**-toh
Is it ready?	È pronto?	eh **prohn**-toh

IT'S NOT WORKING!

This room is cold/hot.	La camera è fredda /calda.	lah **kah**-meh-rah **eh**-**frehd**-dah/**kahl**-dah
The...is not working.	*...non funziona.*	*nohn foon-**tsyoh**-nah*
air conditioning	l'aria condizionata	**lah**-ree-ah kohn-dee-tsyoh-**nah**-tah
electric socket	la presa della corrente	lah **preh**-zah **dehl**-lah kohr-**rehn**-teh
electricity	la corrente	lah kohr-**rehn**-teh
fan	il ventilatore	eel vehn-tee-lah-**toh**-reh
faucet	il rubinetto	eel roo-bee-**neht**-toh
heating	il riscaldamento	eel ree-skahl-dah-**mehn**-toh
hot water	l'acqua calda	**lah**-kwah **kahl**-dah

light switch	l'interruttore	leen-tehr-root-**toh**-reh
light	la luce	lah **loo**-cheh
television	il televisore	eel teh-leh-vee-**zoh**-reh
The wash basin is blocked.	il lavandino è bloccato.	eel lah-vahn-**dee**-noh eh blohk-**kah**-toh.
The window/door is jammed.	la finestra/la porta non apra/non chiude.	lah **fee**-neh-strah/lah **pohr**-tah nohn **ah**-prah /nohn **kyoo**-deh
There is a bad odor.	C'è un cattivo odore.	cheh oon kaht-**tee**-voh oh-**doh**-reh

ROOM SERVICE

What time is...?	*A che ora è...*	*ah keh* ***oh****-rah eh*
breakfast	la colazione	lah koh-lah-**tsyoh**-neh
lunch	il pranzo	eel **prahn**-zoh
dinner	la cena	lah **cheh**-nah
We'll have breakfast in the room.	Faremo colazione in camera.	fah-**reh**-moh koh-lah-**tsyoh**-neh een **kah**-meh-rah
Breakfast for room #...	La colazione per la camera numero...	lah koh-lah-**tsyoh**-neh pehr lah **kah**-meh-rah **noo**-meh-roh
Please wake me at...	*Per favore mi svegli alle...*	*pehr fah-****voh****-reh mee* ***zveh****-lyee* ***ahl****-leh*
6:00 a.m.	sei del mattino	**seh**-ee dehl maht-**tee**-noh
6:30 a.m.	sei e mezzo	**seh**-ee eh **mehd**-zoh
7:00 a.m.	sette del mattino	**seht**-teh dehl maht-**tee**-noh
7:30 a.m.	sette e mezzo	**seht**-teh eh **mehd**-zoh

AT THE DOOR

Who is it?	Chi è?	kee **eh**
Just a minute.	Un momento.	oon moh-**mehn**-toh.
Come in.	Entri (venga).	**ehn**-tree (**vehn**-gah)
Put it on the table. Thank you.	Lo metta sul tavolo. Grazie.	loh **meht**-teh sool **tah**-voh-loh, **grah**-tsyeh

TELEPHONE

Pay phones are found in most public places, bars, cafés, air and train terminals. Public phones are used for local and intercity calls. To make an international call, you will need to find **il telefono di stato**. Call collect or use a telephone credit card. Hotels will usually add a surcharge on international calls unless you are using a calling card.

Public phones use **gettoni** or **la carta telefonica**. Have your change ready or purchase a telephone card. If you are using tokens, you will be asked to deposit as many as needed or you will hear a beep when the time is up. Some phones still operate on clicking timers. You will be charged by the numbers of clicks or **scatti**. An electronic phone card will give you a read-out of how many lira are left on your card. To make a hotel reservation or a business call in Italian, a hotel clerk will help you if you feel you will not be able to make yourself understood. For information in English, dial 176.

When calling, you'll notice the signals are different from those in North America. Two long *too, too* sounds signify ringing and a connection. Three short *too, too, too* sounds indicate the line is busy.

In Italian, phone numbers are usually read in two-digit combinations and are rarely read digit after digit, as they are in English.

78-45-1 (seventy-eight, forty-five, one)	settantotto quarantacinque uno	seht-tahnt-**oht**-toh kwah-rahn-tah-**cheen**-kweh **oo**-noh
24-88-52 (twenty-four, eighty-eight, fifty-two)	ventiquattro ottantotto cinquantadue	vehn-tee-**kwaht**-troh oht-tahnt-**oht**-toh cheen-**kwahn**-tah-doo-eh
#345 (Extension) (three hundred, forty-five)	trecento quarantacinque	treh-**chehn**-toh kwah-rahn-tah-**cheen**-kweh

Where is the...?	*Dov'è...?*	***doh-veh***
telephone	il telefono	eel teh-**leh**-foh-noh
public telephone	il telefono pubblico	eel teh-**leh**-foh-noh **poo**-blee-koh
telephone book	un elenco telefonico	oon eh-**lehn**-koh teh-leh-**foh**-nee-koh
Are tokens needed for the telephone?	Occorrono i gettoni per il telefono?	ohk-**kohr**-roh-noh ee jeht-**toh**-nee pehr eel teh-leh-**foh**-noh
Please,...	*Per favore,...*	*pehr fah-**voh**-reh*
the telephone number of...	il numero di telefono di...	eel **noo**-meh-roh dee tel-leh-**foh**-noh dee
connect me with number...	la camera numero...	lah **kah**-meh-rah **noo**-meh-roh
information	il servizio informazioni	eel sehr-**vee**-tsyoh een-fohr-mah-**tsyoh**-nee
long distance	la centralinista	lah chehn-trah-lee-**nee**-stah
international operator	l'operatore internazionale	loh-peh-rah-**toh**-reh enn-tehr-nah-tsyoh-**nah**-leh
I'd like to make...	*Vorrei fare una telefonata...*	*vohr-**ray** **fah**-reh **oo**-nah teh-leh-foh-**nah**-tah*
a collect call	a carico al destinatario	ah **kah**-ree-koh ahl deh-stee-nah-**tah**-ree-oh
a local call	urbana	oor-**bah**-nah
a long-distance call	interurbana	een-tehr-oor-**bah**-nah
an overseas call	internazionale	een-tehr-nah-tsyoh-**nah**-leh
a person-to-person call	con preavviso	kohn preh-ah-**vee**-zoh
What is the area code for...?	Qual è il prefisso per...?	kwahl-**eh** eel preh-**fees**-soh pehr
I'd like to use my credit card.	Vorrei usare la mia carta di credito.	vohr-**ray** oo-**zah**-reh lah **mee**-ah **kahr**-tah dee **kreh**-dee-toh

How much per minute?	Quanto devo pagare?	**kwahn**-toh **deh**-voh pah-**gah**-reh
How long must I wait?	Quanto devo aspettare?	**kwahn**-toh **deh**-voh ahs-peh-**tah**-reh
My number is...	Il mio numero è...	eel **mee**-oh **noo**-meh-roh eh
Do you speak English?	Parla inglese?	**pahr**-lah een-**gleh**-zeh

What you may hear

Pronto! Chi parla?	**prohn**-toh. kee **pahr**-lah	Hello! Who's speaking?
Sono... (parla...).	**soh**-noh (**pahr**-lah)	This is...(speaking).
Non risponde nessuno.	nohn ree-**spohn**-deh nehs-**soo**-noh	There's no answer.
Non si sente bene.	nohn see **sehn**-teh **beh**-neh	I cannot hear you.
Ha sbagliato il numero.	ah sbah-**lyah**-toh eel **noo**-meh-roh	You've got the wrong number.
Rimanga in linea.	ree-**mahn**-gah een **lee**-neh-ah	Please wait.
La linea è occupata.	lah **lee**-neh-ah eh ohk-koo-**pah**-tah	The line is busy.
È caduta la linea.	eh kah-**doo**-tah lah **lee**-neh-ah	The line was cut off.
Rifaccio il numero?	ree-**fah**-chyoh eel **noo**-meh-roh	Please call back.
Pronto!	**prohn**-toh	Yes. (I'm listening.)
Non riattacchi (agganci).	nohn reet-**tahk**-kee (ah-**gahn**-chee)	Don't hang up.
Il telefono non funziona.	eel teh-leh-**foh**-noh nohn foon-**tsyoh**-nah	The telephone doesn't work.
Si è interrotta la comunicazione.	see eh een-tehr-**roht**-tah lah koh-moo-nee-kah-**tsyoh**-neh	Your call was disconnected.
Desidera che continui a provare?	deh-**zee**-deh-rah keh kohn-**tee**-noo-ee ah proh-**vah**-reh	Would you like to keep trying?

IF ALL ELSE FAILS

May I speak to...?	Posso parlare con...?	**pohs**-soh pahr-**lah**-re kohn
I don't understand.	Non capisco.	nohn kah-**pee**-skoh
Please speak more slowly.	Parli più adagio, per favore.	**pahr**-lee pyoo ah-**dah**-jyoh, pehr fah-**voh**-reh
Does anyone speak English?	C'è qualcuno che parla inglese?	cheh kwahl-**koo**-noh keh **pahr**-lah een-**gleh**-zeh

CHECKING OUT

What time is check-out?	A che ora devo lasciare la camera?	ah keh **oh**-rah **deh**-voh lah-**shyah**-reh lah **kah**-mehr-rah
I'm (we're) leaving...	*Partirò (Partiremo)...*	*pahr-tee-**roh** (pahr-tee-**reh**-moh)*
this afternoon	questo pomeriggio	**kweh**-stoh poh-meh-**reej**-jyoh
tomorrow morning	domani mattina	doh-**mah**-nee maht-**tee**-nah
tonight	stasera	stah-**seh**-rah
Please have my bill ready.	Per favore, prepari il conto.	pehr fah-**voh**-reh, preh-**pah**-ree eel **kohn**-toh
Is this correct?	È tutto a posto?	eh **toot**-toh ah **poh**-stoh
Everything is okay.	Si, tutto a posto.	see, **toot**-toh ah **poh**-stoh
I'll need a porter.	Per favore, mandi qualcuno a prendere le valigie.	pehr fah-**voh**-reh, **mahn**-dee ah **prehn**-deh-reh leh vah-**lee**-jyeh

POST OFFICE

Where is the post office?	Dov'̀e l'ufficio postale?	doh-veh loo-fee-chyoh poh stah-leh
Where is the mail box?	Dov'è una casetta postale?	doh-veh oo-nah kah-seht-tah poh-stah-leh?
How much for stamps to Canada?	Quanti francobolli per Canada?	kwahn-tee frahn-koh-bohl-lee pehr eel Kah-nah-dah?

Write a few words to your friends in Italian

Caro (**kah**-roh - male friend)...,	Dear...,
Cara (**kah**-rah - female friend)...,	
Saluti! (sah-**loo**-tee)	Greetings!
Come stai? (**koh**-meh **stah**-ee)	How are things?
*Saluti (sah-**loo**-tee)*	*Greetings from...*
da Roma (dah **Roh**-mah)	Rome
da Firenze (dah Fee-**rehn**-seh)	Florence
d'all'Italia (dahl-ee-**tah**-lee-ah)	Italy
Auguri! (Ow-**goo**-ree!)	All the best!

Look for the **PT** sign (**Poste e Telecommunicazione**). Mail delivery is slow from Italy, so be sure to weigh any letters or parcels. They will be returned for insufficient postage. Mail boxes are red and located outside the post offices and tobacco shops. Be sure to post your letter in the correct box, not the one marked "CITT À".

CHAPTER SEVEN

Dining out

Eating in Italy is a delight, but can be very expensive. Before you dine, check the menus posted outside each restaurant. These explain the **servizio** (service charge) and the **coperto** (cover charge). In the main piazza, expect to pay top price. Enjoy the atmosphere and sip slowly...

Your hotel concierge is the best source for information on good, authentic and out-of-the-way places to eat. Ask any group of Italians, "Where can you eat well?" — "**Dove si mangia bene?**" (Doh-veh see **mahn**-jyah **beh**-neh?) and they will instantly become animated and tell you their favorite place to eat.

In bars and freeway rest stops, you generally pay first at the **cassa** and take your receipt to the counter to order. There are generally two prices posted, one for the stand-up bar and one for a table. Here you can get a quick bite. Be sure to sample **i tost** (ee tohst), a version of our sandwich with an extensive variety of fillings. Lunch is served between 12:30 and 3:00 p.m. Most places will not serve dinner before 7:00 p.m and serve as late as 10:00 p.m.

This chapter includes a food dictionary, divided into various food groups in alphabetical order. The list of foods is as varied as Italian cuisine. This will assist you in reading an Italian menu or allow your server to point to the dish on the menu.

"BUON APPETITO" - "HAVE A PLEASANT MEAL!"

WHERE TO EAT?

AUTOGRILL	A self-service cafeteria on the Autostrade, with bar, restaurant, market, souvenirs, telephones.
BAR/CAFFÈ	Espresso, cappuccino, ice cream, pastries, sandwiches, some alcoholic drinks; usually quick, stand-up meals.
TRATTORIA/OSTERIA	Moderately priced but excellent local dishes; rustic, informal often family-operated.
TAVOLA CALDA/FREDDA	Small, self-serve restaurant serving hot and cold dishes, moderately priced.
ROSTICCERIA	Specializing in take-out roasted meats; many have seating to stay and enjoy.
PIZZERIA	Pizzas of every variety; small, family operated; other dishes available.
RISTORANTE	Elegant, more expensive; rated for its food and decor; preview the menu posted in the window.
GELATERIA	Ice cream parlor.
PANINOTECA	A great variety of panini, sandwiches; served hot (toasted in a special grill) or cold.

I'm hungry.	Ho fame.	oh **fah**-meh
I'm thirsty.	Ho sete.	oh **seh**-teh
Where can you eat well?	Dove si mangia bene?	**doh**-veh see **mahn**-jyah **beh**-neh
Do you know a good restaurant?	Conosce un buon ristorante?	koh-**noh**-sheh oon **bwohn** ree-stoh-**rahn**-teh
I would like a ...restaurant.	*Vorrei un ristorante...*	*vohr-**ray** oon ree-stoh-**rahn**-teh*
typical (of the region)	tipico	**tee**-pee-koh
very good	molto buono	**mohl**-toh **bwoh**-noh
Do you need a reservation?	Si deve prenotare?	see **deh**-veh preh-noh-**tah**-reh

Is it expensive?	È molto costoso?	eh **mohl**-toh koh-**stoh**-soh
No, it's inexpensive.	Non, è economico.	nohn, eh eh-koh-**noh**-mee-**koh**
What's the restaurant called?	Come si chiama il ristorante?	**koh**-meh see **kyah**-mah eel ree-stoh-**rahn**-teh
Where is it located?	Dove si trova?	**doh**-veh see **troh**-vah
Is it close/far?	È vicino / lontano?	eh vee-**chee**-noh/lohn-**tah**-noh
I would like to make a reservation...	*Vorrei fare una prenotazione...*	*vohr-**ray** **fah**-reh **oo**-nah preh-noh-tah-**tsyoh**-neh*
for tonight	per stasera	pehr stah-**seh**-rah
for tomorrow evening	per domani sera	pehr doh-**mah**-nee
for two (four, six)	per due (quattro, sei) persone	pehr **doo**-eh (**kwaht**-troh, **seh**-ee) pehr-**soh**-neh
inside	dentro	**dehn**-troh
outside	all'aperto (fuori)	ahl-ah-**pehr**-toh (**fwoh**-ree)

ORDERING

We'd like to have lunch (dinner) now.	Vorremmo pranzare adesso.	vohr-**rehm**-moh prahn-**zah**-reh ah-**dehs**-soh
I (we) would like a table for...two (three, four).	Una tavola per due, (tre, quattro), per favore.	**oo**-nah **tah**-voh-lah pehr **doo**-eh (treh, **kwaht**-troh), pehr fah-**voh**-reh
Waiter!	Cameriere!	**kah**-mehr-yeh-reh!
Is this spot taken?	È libero?	eh **lee**-beh-roh
The menu, please.	Il menù, per piacere.	eel meh-**noo**, pehr pyah-**cheh**-reh
The wine list, please.	La lista dei vini, per piacere.	lah **lee**-stah day **vee**-nee, pehr pyah-**cheh**-reh
I'd (We'd) like to order now.	Vorrei (vorremmo) ordinare adesso.	vohr-**ray** (vohr-**rehm**-moh) ohr-dee-**nah**-reh ah-**dehs**-soh

I would like (We would like)...	*Vorrei (Vorremmo)...*	*vohr-**ray** (vohr-**rehm**-moh)*
the set meal	il menu turistico	eel meh-**noo** too-**ree**-stee-koh
today's special	il piatto(menù) del giorno	eel **pyaht**-toh (meh-**noo**) dehl **jyohr**-noh
something light	qualcosa di leggero	kwahl-**koh**-sah dee lehj-**jeh**-roh
a full meal	un pasto completo	oon **pah**-stoh kohm-**pleh**-toh
What's the house specialty?	Qual'è la specialità della casa?	kwahl-**eh** lah speh-chyah-lee-**tah** **dehl**-lah **kah**-sah
Do you have children's portions?	Avete mezze porzioni per bambini?	ah-**veh**-teh **mehd**-zeh pohr-**tsyoh**-nee pehr bahm-**bee**-nee
I'm not very hungry.	Non ho molta fame.	nohn oh **mohl**-toh **fah**-meh
I would only like...	*Vorrei solo...*	*vohr-**ray** **soh**-loh*
a sandwich	un tramezzino	oon trah-mehd-**zee**-noh
a first course	il primo	eel **pree**-moh
a main course	il secondo	eel seh-**kohn**-doh
a snack	uno spuntino	oon-oh spoon-**tee**-noh
Are the portions large or small?	Le porzioni sono piccole o grandi?	leh pohr-**tsyoh**-nee **soh**-noh **peek**-koh-lee oh **grahn**-dee
To start, bring us...	*Per cominciare, ci porti...*	*pehr koh-meen-**chyah**-reh, chee **pohr**-tee*
an apéritif	un aperitivo	oon ah-peh-ree-**tee**-voh
a beer	una birra	**oo**-nah **beer**-rah
a cocktail	un cocktail	oon kohk-**tayl**
some white/red wine	del vino bianco/rosso	dehl **vee**-noh **byahn**-koh/**rohs**-soh

To start, bring us...	*Per cominciare, ci porti...*	*pehr koh-meen-**chyah**-reh, chee **pohr**-tee*
a litre (half litre) of house wine	un litro (mezzo litro) del vino di casa	oon lee-troh (**mehd**-zoh **leet**-troh) dehl **vee**-noh **dee**-lah **kah**-sah
some water	dell'acqua	dehl-**ah**-kwah
a bottle of mineral carbonated (natural) water	una bottiglia d'acqua minerale gassata (naturale)	**oo**-nah boht-**tee**-lyah **dah**-kwah mee-neh-**rah**-leh gahs-**sah**-tah (nah-too-**rah**-leh)
Cheers/ To our health!	Chin! Chin / Salute!	cheen cheen sah-**loo**-teh
Next...	Poi...	poy
Finally...	Per finire...	pehr fee-**nee**-reh
Nothing else, thank you.	È tutto, grazie.	eh **toot**-toh, **grah**-tsyeh

DIETARY RESTRICTIONS

I have an allergy.	Sono allergico(-a) a...	**soh**-noh ahl-**lehr**-jee-koh (-a) ah
I'm on a special diet.	Seguo una dieta speciale.	**seh**-gwoh **oo**-nah dee-**eh**-tah speh-**chyah**-leh
I can't eat anything made with... (or)	Non posso mangiare niente fatto con...	nohn **pohs**-soh mahn-**jyah**-reh **nyehn**-teh **faht**-toh kohn
I don't eat...	*Non mangio...*	*nohn **mahn**-jyoh*
dairy	prodotti casearei	proh-**doht**-tee kah-zeh-**ah**-reh-ee
eggs	le uova	leh **woh**-vah
fat	i grassi	ee **grahs**-see
fried food	cose fritte	**koh**-zeh **freet**-teh
flour (wheat)	la farina	lah fah-**ree**-nah
meat	il carne	eel **kahr**-neh
nuts	le noci	leh **noh**-chee
salt	il sale	eel **sah**-leh
sugar	lo zucchero	loh **dzook**-keh-roh

I don't drink alcohol.	Non bevo le bevande alcoliche.	nohn **beh**-voh leh beh-**vahn**-deh ahl-**koh**-lee-keh
I'm diabetic.	Ho il diabete.	oh eel dee-ah-**beh**-teh
Can I have saccharin?	Potrei avere della saccarina?	poh-**tray** ah-**veh**-reh **dehl**-lah sahk-kah-**ree**-nah
I don't eat pork.	Non mangio carne di maiale.	nohn **mahn**-jyoh **kahr**-neh dee mah-**yah**-leh
Do you have vegetarian dishes?	Servite piatti vegetariani?	sehr-**vee**-teh **pyaht**-tee veh-geh-tah-ree-**ah**-nee

PROBLEMS

I didn't order this.	Non è quello che avevo ordinato.	nohn **eh** **kwehl**-loh keh ah-**veh**-voh ohr-dee-**nah**-toh
This dish is (too)...	*È (troppo)...*	*eh (**trohp**-poh)*
cold	freddo	**frehd**-doh
inedible	immangiabile	eem-mahn-**jyah**-bee-leh
overcooked	cotto	**koht**-toh
rare, undercooked	al sangue	ahl **sahn**-gweh
salty	salato	sah-**lah**-toh
spicy	piccante	peek-**kahn**-teh
sweet	dolce	**dohl**-cheh
tough	duro	**doo**-roh
I don't like it.	Non mi piace.	nohn mee **pyah**-cheh
This is not clean.	Non è pulito.	nohn **eh** poo-**lee**-toh
This is not fresh.	Non è fresco.	nohn **eh** **freh**-skoh
Please bring us (a, an)...	*Per piacere, ci porti...*	*pehr pyah-**cheh**-reh, chee **pohr**-tee*
another place setting	delle posate	**dehl**-leh poh-**sah**-teh
ashtray	una portacenere	**oo**-nah pohr-tah-**cheh**-neh-reh
cup	una tazza	**oo**-nah **taht**-tsah
fork	una forchetta	oo-nah fohr-**keht**-tah
glass	un bicchiere	oon bee-**kyeh**-reh
knife	un coltello	oon kohl-**tehl**-loh

Please bring us (a, an)...	*Per piacere, ci porti...*	*pehr pyah-**cheh**-reh, chee **pohr**-tee*
napkin	un tovagliolo	oon tah-voh-**lyoh**-loh
plate	un piatto	oon **pyaht**-toh
saucer	un piattino	oon pyaht-**tee**-noh
spoon	un cucchiaio	oon kook-**kyah**-yoh
teaspoon	un cucchiaino	oon kook-kyah-**ee**-noh
toothpick	uno stuzzicadenti	**oo**-noh stoot-tsee-kah-**dehn**-tee

Could we have some...?	*Potremmo avere...?*	*poh-**traym**-moh ah-**veh**-reh*
bread	del pane	dehl **pah**-neh
butter	del burro	dehl **boor**-roh
horseradish	del rafano	dehl **rah**-fah-noh
ketchup	del ketchup	dehl **kehch**-ahp
lemon	del limone	dehl lee-**moh**-neh
margarine	della margarina	**dehl**-lah mahr-gah-**ree**-nah
mayonnaise	della maionese	**dehl**-lah may-oh-**nay**-seh
mustard	della senape, mostarda	**dehl**-lah **seh**-nah-peh, moh-**stahr**-dah
olive oil	olio d'oliva	**oh**-lee-oh doh-**lee**-vah
pepper (black)	del pepe (nero)	dehl **peh**-peh (**neh**-roh)
(red)	(rosso)	(**rohs**-soh)
(hot peppers)	(peperoni)	(peh-peh-**roh**-nee)
salt	del sale	dehl **sah**-leh
sugar	dello zucchero	**dehl**-loh **dzook**-keh-roh
vinegar	dell' aceto	dehl ah-**cheh**-toh
A little more, please.	Ancora un po', per piacere.	ahn-**koh**-rah oon **poh** pehr pyah-**cheh**-reh

PAYING THE BILL

A surcharge for service is normally included in the bill. Tips are usually 10-15% for courteous service, otherwise 10% at your discretion.

The cheque, please.	Il conto, per favore.	eel **kohn**-toh pehr fah-**voh**-reh

We're in a hurry.	Siamo in fretta.	see-**ah**-moh een **freht**-tah
Separate cheques, please.	Conti separati, per cortesia.	**kohn**-tee seh-pah-**rah**-tee pehr kohr-teh-**see**-yah
We're splitting the cheque (literally, "going Roman")	Facciamo alla romana.	fah-**chyah**-moh **ahl**-lah roh-**mah**-nah
Is the service included?	Il servizio è compreso?	eel sehr-**vee**-tsyoh eh kohm-**preh**-soh
Is the bread and cover charge included in the price?	Pane e coperto sono compresi nel prezzo?	**pah**-neh eh koh-**pehr**-toh **soh**-noh kohm-**preh**-zee nehl **preht**-tsoh?
I don't think the bill is correct.	Non penso che il conto sia corretto.	nohn **pehn**-soh keh eel **kohn**-toh **see**-ah kohr-**reht**-toh
What's this amount for?	Per che cos'è quest'importo?	pehr keh kohs-**eh** **kwehst**-eem-**pohrt**-toh
The service was very good.	Il servizio è stato ottimo.	eel sehr-**vee**-tsyoh eh **stah**-toh **oht**-tee-moh
The meal was delicious.	È stato un pasto delizioso.	eh **stah**-toh oon **pah**-stoh deh-lee-**tsyoh**-zoh
This is for you.	Questo è per lei.	**kweh**-stoh **eh** pehr **lay**

What you may hear

Cosa desidera?	What would you like to order?
Oggi Le consiglio...	I recommend...
La specialità della casa è...	This is our special dish.
Desidera qualcosa da bere?	What would you like to drink?
Per cominciare?	What would you like to start?
Cosa desidera di secondo?	What would you like as a main course?
E di contorno?	And, as a side dish?
Mi dispiace, ... è finito.	I'm sorry, we're out of...
Buon appetito!	Bon appétit!
È tutto a posto?	Is everything alright?
Ci vuole...minuti per preparazione.	It will take...minutes (to prepare).

From the menu, it may not be clear how the food is prepared. Construct your own questions in Italian using **È...? - Is this...?** Or, you may specify how you would like your meal prepared: **Preferisco...**

Is this fresh?	**È** fresco?	eh **freh**-skoh?
I prefer it broiled.	**Preferisco** alla graticola.	preh-feh-**ree**-skoh **ahl**-lah grah-tee-**koh**-lah

Is this...?	*È...?*	*eh*
baked	al forno	ahl **fohr**-noh
barbecued	ai ferri	**ah**-ee **fehr**-ree
bitter	amaro	ah-**mah**-roh
boiled	lesso	**lehs**-soh
braised	brasato	brah-**zah**-toh
broiled	alla graticola	**ahl**-lah grah-tee-**koh**-lah
broiled on a spit	allo spiedo	**ahl**-loh **spyeh**-doh
cold	freddo	**frehd**-doh
fresh	fresco	**freh**-skoh
fried	fritto	**freet**-toh
grilled	alla griglia	**ahl**-lah **gree**-lyah
marinated	marinato	mah-ree-**nah**-toh
poached	affogato	ahf-foh-**gah**-toh
roasted	arrosto	ahr-**roh**-stoh
salty	salato	sah-**lah**-toh
sautéed	saltato	sahl-**tah**-toh
sealed in parchment	al cartoccio	ahl kahr-**toh**-chyoh
spicy	piccante	peek-**kahn**-teh
steamed	al vapore	ahl vah-**poh**-reh
stewed	in umido	een **oo**-mee-doh
stuffed	farcito	fahr-**chee**-toh
sweet	dolce	**dohl**-cheh
tough	duro	**doo**-roh

Use the following expression to describe the food: **Questo è (troppo)**... or **Questo (non) è**...

This is (not)...	*Questo (non) è...*	***kweh**-stoh (nohn) eh*
This is (too)...	*Questo è (troppo)...*	***kweh**-stoh eh (**trohp**-poh)*

FOOD DICTIONARY

The sample menu items below are listed by category and alphabetically in Italian. Italian menus vary region to region and change depending on the season. The variety is endless.

The lists below allow you to quickly match up and find what you may want to order. It will also allow you to ask questions if you have specific food allergies, or allow your server to point.

Remember, you can always use "Please, I would like..." – "**Per favore, vorrei...**" (Pehr fah-**voh**-reh, vohr-**ray...**) with your request. Don't worry about gender, articles and endings. Just say it in Italian!

Antipasti (ahn-tee-**pah**-stee)

In Italian cuisine, appetizers are more popular in the summer. They may be hot or cold, and consist of raw salads, cooked chilled vegetables and an endless variety of salamis and sausages. Tables of antipasti may be set up from which you may choose combination plates, simply by pointing.

Appetizers	***Antipasti***	
assorted appetizers	antipasto misto	ahn-tee-**pah**-stoh **mee**-stoh
assorted cold cuts	affettato misto	ahf-feht-**tah**-toh mee-stoh
fresh mozzarella cheese, sliced with tomatoes, basil, olive oil	caprese	kah-**preh**-seh

Appetizers	***Antipasti***	
thinly sliced raw beef with oil, lemon, flakes of parmesan cheese	carpaccio	kahr-**pah**-chyoh
shrimp cocktail	cocktail di gamberi	kohk-**tayl** dee **gahm**-beh-ree
mussels in tomato garlic sauce	cozze alla marinara	**koht**-tseh **ahl**-lah mah-ree-**nah**-rah
seafood salad with clams, mussels, squid, prawns, lemon	insalata di frutti di mare	een-sah-**lah**-tah dee **froot**-teh dee **mah**-reh
dry-cured prosciutto ham with melon or figs	prosciutto e melone o fichi	proh-**shoot**-toh eh meh-**loh**-neh oh **fee**-kee

Soups	***Zuppa***	
...broth	*brodo...*	***broh**-doh*
capon	di cappone	dee kah-**poh**-neh
beef	di manzo	dee **mahn**-zoh
chicken	di pollo	dee **pohl**-loh
cream...soup	*crema...*	***kreh**-mah*
of asparagus	di asparagi	dee ah-**spah**-rah-jee
of mushroom	di funghi	dee **foon**-ghee
of tomato	di pomodoro	dee poh-moh-**doh**-roh
vegetable soup	minestrone	mee-neh-**stroh**-neh
cream of pea soup	passato di piselli	pahs-**sah**-toh dee pee-**zehl**-lee
cream of vegetable soup	passato di verdura	pahs-**sah**-toh dee vehr-**doo**-rah
pasta and bean soup	pasta e fagioli	**pah**-stah eh fah-**jyoh**-lee
broth with tiny pasta	pastina in brodo	pah-**stee**-nah een **broh**-doh
broth with egg and cheese	stracciatella	strah-chyah-**tehl**-lah
seafood stew	zuppa di pesce	**dzoop**-pah dee **peh**-sheh

FIRST COURSE *I PRIMI PIATTI*
Pasta, Risotto, Polenta e Gnocchi

There are as many theories about the origins of **pasta (pah**-stah) in Italy as there are varieties and ways of preparing this most popular of Italian dishes. The most commonly held theory is that Marco Polo first brought back pasta to Italy from the East. Despite the fact that there are references to pasta as far back as the times of Cicero, it is said that during his voyage, Marco Polo sent one of his sailors ashore in search of fresh water. There the sailor witnessed a native woman cooking long strands of food in boiling water and acquired the secret recipe. The sailor's name was none other than Spaghetti!

Riso, or **risotto**, most popular in Northern Italy, is prepared with broth or with a variety of ingredients. Its creamy texture flavored by porcini (pohr-**chee**-nee) mushrooms, for example, is well worth the wait. **Polenta** (poh-**lehn**-tah) is cooked cornmeal, served sliced and grilled, with stews or sauces. **Gnocchi (nyohk**-kee) are small potato dumplings, made sometimes with spinach or squash, served with meat or tomato sauces.

tiny, round ravioli, stuffed with meat or cheese	agnolotti	ah-nyoh-**loht**-tee
large, rolled pasta filled with meat or spinach and ricotta, baked in white sauce	cannelloni	kahn-nehl-**loh**-nee
"little-hats" round-shaped pasta filled with chopped chicken, ham, cheese and eggs	cappelletti	kahp-peh-**leht**-tee
flat noodles	fettuccine	feht-too-**chee**-neh
small potato dumplings, made sometimes with spinach or squash	gnocchi	**nyohk**-kee
baked layers of thin pasta with white sauce, meat sauce and cheese	lasagne	lah-**sah**-nyeh

baked layers of thin spinach pasta with white sauce, meat sauce and cheese	lasagne verde	lah-**sah**-nyeh **vehr**-deh
pasta squares filled with chopped chicken, spinach, ricotta or ground meat	ravioli	rah-**vyoh**-lee
large, ridged tubular pasta	rigatoni	ree-gah-**toh**-nee
thin, solid strands	spaghetti	spah-**gheht**-tee
flat, narrow strips	tagliatelle	tah-lyah-**tehl**-leh
pasta rings filled with chopped chicken, spinach, ricotta or ground meat	tortellini	tohr-tehl-**lee**-nee
omelette, often filled with vegetables	frittata	freet-**tah**-tah
rice with green peas and bacon	risi bisi	**ree**-zee **bee**-zee
boiled rice with butter and grated cheese	riso in bianco	**ree**-zoh een **byahn**-koh
rice with tomato sauce and herbs	riso al pomodoro	**ree**-zoh ahl poh-moh-**doh**-roh
rice boiled with broth	risotto	ree-**zoht**-toh
with seafood	alla marinara	**ahl**-lah mah-ree-**nah**-rah
with saffron	alla milanese	**ahl**-lah mee-lah-**neh**-seh

Sauces

garlic, olive oil and red pepper	aglio, olio e peperoncino	**ah**-lyoh, **oh**-lyoh eh peh-peh-rohn-**chee**-noh
tomatoes, bacon, garlic, red peppers, onions	all'amatriciana	**ahl**-ah-mah-tree-**chyah**-nah
tomatoes, ground meat with red wine and a dash of milk or cream	alla bolognese/al ragù	**ahl**-lah boh-loh-**nyeh**-zeh /ahl rah-**goo**
with eggs, ham, bacon and cheese	alla carbonara	**ahl**-lah kahr-boh-**nah**-rah

tomatoes, mussels and clams	alla marinara	**ahl**-lah mah-ree-**nah**-rah
ground basil, pine nuts, garlic, cheese and oil	al pesto	ahl **peh**-stoh
pureed tomatoes, garlic, olive oil and herbs	al pomodoro	ahl poh-moh-**doh**-roh
olives, garlic, capers, red dried peppers and oil	alla puttanesca	**ahl**-lah poot-tah-**neh**-skah
tomatoes, clams, parsley, garlic	alle vongole	**ahl**-leh **vohn**-goh-leh
white sauce made with butter, flour, cream and milk	besciamella	beh-shyah-**mehl**-lah

Pizza

Pizze (pizzas) in Italy are usually made for one and are as large as a dinner plates. **Pizzerie** (pizza parlors) offer a wide variety of toppings that are quite different from North American ingredients.

filled pizza pastry, baked or deep fried	calzone	kahl-**tsoh**-neh
tomato, mozzarella, ham, mushrooms, artichoke hearts	capricciosa	kah-pree-**chyoh**-zah
tomato, mozzarella, basil	margherita	mahr-gheh-**ree**-tah
tomato, garlic, oregano	marinara	mah-ree-**nah**-rah
tomato, mozzarella, anchovies, oregano	napoletana	nah-poh-leh-**tah**-nah
tomato, mozzarella, ham, sausage, mushrooms, artichoke hearts, separated into quarters	quattro stagioni (the "four seasons")	**kwah**-troh stah-**jyoh**-neh
tomato, mozzarella, anchovies, oregano, capers	romana	roh-**mah**-nah
tomatoes, anchovies, pecorino cheese	siciliana	see-chee-**lyah**-nah

MAIN COURSES — *I SECONDI PIATTI*

Fish & Seafood	***Pesce***	
anchovies	acciughe	ah-**chyoo**-gheh
lobster	aragosta	ah-rah-**goh**-stah
salt-dried cod	baccalà	bahk-kah-**lah**
squid	calamari	kah-lah-**mah**-ree
mussels	cozze	**koht**-tseh
shrimps	gamberi	**gahm**-beh-ree
crabs	granchi	**grahn**-kee
oysters	ostriche	**oh**-stree-keh
swordfish	pesce spada	**peh**-sheh **spah**-dah
octopus	polipo	**poh**-lee-poh
sole	sogliola	**soh**-lyoh-lah
clams	vongole	**vohn**-goh-leh

Meat	***Carne***	
lamb	agnello	ahn-**nyehl**-loh
steak	bistecca	bee-**stehk**-kah
chop	braciola	brah-**chyoh**-lah
rib	costoletta	koh-stoh-**leht**-tah
cutlet	cotoletta	koh-toh-**leht**-tah
liver	fegato	**feh**-gah-toh
tongue	lingua	**leen**-gwah
pork	maiale	mah-**yah**-leh
beef	manzo	**mahn**-zoh
bologna	mortadella	mohr-tah-**dehl**-lah
bacon (smoked)	pancetta (affumicata)	pahn-**cheht**-tah
meat balls	polpette	pohl-**peht**-teh
suckling pig	porchetta	pohr-**keht**-tah
dry-cured ham	prosciutto	proh-**shoot**-toh
roast beef	rosbif	rohs-**beef**
salami	salame	sah-**lah**-meh
sausage	salsiccia	sahl-**see**-chyah
thin slices	scaloppine	skah-lohp-**pee**-neh
veal	vitello	vee-**tehl**-loh

Poultry & Game	***Pollo***	
capon	cappone	kahp-**poh**-neh
venison	carne di cervo	**kahr**-neh dee **chehr**-voh
rabbit	coniglio	koh-**nee**-lyoh
pheasant	fagiano	fah-**jyah**-noh
chicken	pollo	**pohl**-loh
turkey	taccino	tahk-**kee**-noh
Vegetables	***Vegetali***	
beets	barbabietole	bahr-bah-**byeh**-toh-leh
artichokes	carciofi	kahr-**chyoh**-fee
cauliflower	cavolfiore	kah-voh-lee-**fyoh**-ree
cabbage	cavolo	**kah**-voh-loh
cucumber	cetriolo	cheh-tree-**oh**-loh
onion	cipolla	chee-**pohl**-lah
beans	fagioli	fah-**jyoh**-lee
fennel	finocchio	fee-**nohk**-kyoh
mushrooms	funghi	**foon**-ghee
mixed salad	insalata mista	een-sah-**lah**-tah **mee**-stah
radicchio salad	insalata di radicchi	een-sah-**lah**-tah dee rah-**deek**-kyoh
cooked potato, vegetable salad with mayonnaise	insalata russa	een-sah-**lah**-tah **roos**-sah
eggplant	melanzana	meh-lahn-**dzah**-nah
potatoes	patate	pah-**tah**-teh
potatoes fried	patatine fritte	pah-**tah**-tee-neh **freet**-teh
peppers	peperoni	peh-peh-**roh**-nee
green peas	piselli	pee-**zehl**-lee
tomatoes	pomodori	poh-moh-**doh**-ree
boletus edulis mushrooms	porcini	pohr-**chee**-nee
truffles	tartufi	tahr-**too**-fee
Fruit	***Frutta***	
apricot	un'albicocca	oon ahl-bee-**kohk**-kah
watermelon	dell'anguria	dehl ahn-**goo**-ree-ah
cherries	delle ciliegie	**dehl**-leh chee-**lyeh**-jeh
figs	dei fichi	day **fee**-kee
strawberries	delle fragole	**dehl**-leh **frah**-goh-leh

Fruit	***Frutta***	
fresh fruit	della frutta fresca	**dehl**-lah **froot**-tah **freh**-skah
lemon	del limone	dehl lee-**moh**-neh
fruit cocktail	una macedonia	**oo**-nah mah-cheh-**doh**-nee-ah
apple	una mela	**oo**-nah **meh**-lah
melon	del melone	dehl meh-**loh**-neh
pear	una pera	**oo**-nah **peh**-rah
peach	una pesca	**oo**-nah **peh**-skah
grapefruit	un pompelmo	oon pohm-**pehl**-moh
Sicilian orange	un tarocco	oon tah-**rohk**-koh

Cheeses - Formaggi

In Italy, there is a variety of cheeses, many of which are not exported. They are served after dinner with fruit and used extensively in cooking. Using the expressions below, you will be able to sample the variety.

Is it a...cheese?	*È un formaggio...?*	*eh oon fohr-**mah**-jyoh*
mild	dolce	**dohl**-cheh
sharp	piccante	peek-**kahn**-teh
hard, aged	duro	**doo**-roh
soft	mollo	**mohl**-loh

Desserts	***Dolci***	
almond macaroons	amaretti	ah-mah-**reht**-tee
custard	crema inglese	**kreh**-mah enn-**gleh**-seh
pie (with fruit in season)	crostata	kroh-**stah**-tah
"a 1,000 leaves" - layers of crisp, buttery pastry with cream	millefoglie	meel-leh-**foh**-lyeh
chocolate truffle	tartufo	tahr-**too**-foh
lady finger cake with moscarpone cheese sprinkled with cocoa	tiramisù	tee-rah-mee-**soo**
chocolate cake	torta al cioccolato	**tohr**-tah ahl chyohk-koh-**lah**-toh

beaten egg yolks, sugar, Marsala wine; served warm or chilled	zabaglione	dzah-bah-**lyoh**-neh

Beverages ***Bevande***

espresso	espresso	eh-sprehs-soh
coffee	*caffè*	***kahf-feh***
with whipped cream	con panna	kohn **pahn**-nah
with a splash of liqueur	coretto	koh-**reht**-toh

Cappuccino gets its name from the color of the habits worn by the Capuchin monks. And remember, **espresso** has no "x."

coffee with hot milk	caffelatte	kahf-feh-**laht**-teh
a longer, weaker espresso	lungo	**loon**-goh
espresso, very strong	ristretto	ree-**streht**-toh
coffee with steamed milk froth	cappuccino	kahp-poo-**chee**-noh
iced	freddo	**frehd**-doh
orange soda	aranciata	ah-rahn-**chyah**-tah
lemonade	limonata	lee-moh-**nah**-tah
carbonated mineral water	acqua minerale gassata	**ah**-kwah mee-neh-**rah**-leh gahs-**sah**-tah
natural mineral water	acqua minerale naturale	**ah**-kwah mee-neh-**rah**-leh nah-too-**rah**-leh
fruit juice	succo di frutta	**sook**-koh dee **froot**-tah
tea	*tè*	*teh*
tea with lemon	con limone	kohn lee-**moh**-neh
tea with milk	con latte	kohn **laht**-teh
iced	freddo	**frehd**-doh
To your health!	Salute!	sah-**loo**-teh
Cheers!	Cin, Cin!	cheen cheen

Alcoholic Beverages	***Bevande alcoliche***	
I would like a bottle of...	*Vorrei una (mezza) bottiglia di...*	*vohr-**ray** **oo**-nah (**mehd**-zah) boht-**tee**-lyah*
I would like a (half) litre of...	*Vorrei un (mezzo) litro di...*	*vohr-**ray** oon (**mehd**-zoh) **lee**-troh dee*
champagne	champagne	shahm-**pahn**
sparkling wine	spumante	spoo-**mahn**-teh
rosé	vino rosé	**vee**-noh roh-**seh**
light wine	vino leggero	**vee**-noh leh-**jeh**-roh
red wine	vino rosso	**vee**-noh **rohs**-soh
white wine	vino bianco	**vee**-noh **byahn**-koh
full-bodied wine	vino corposo	**vee**-noh kohr-**poh**-zoh
dry wine	vino secco	**vee**-noh **sehk**-koh
dessert wine	vino dolce	**vee**-noh **dohl**-cheh
I would like...	*Vorrei...*	*vohr-**ray***
a bitter	un amaro	oon ah-**mah**-roh
a beer	una birra	**oo**-nah **beer**-rah
a brandy	un brandy	oon **brahn**-dee
a digestive	un digestivo	oon dee-jeh-**stee**-voh
a grappa	una grappa	oo-nah **grahp**-pah
a sambuca	una sambuca	**oo**-nah sahm-**book**-kah

CHAPTER EIGHT

Shopping

Welcome to shopper's paradise. Prices are "fixed" (**prezzi fissi**) in most stores, although you may receive a discount on sizeable purchases. Look for end-of-season sales in late August and after Christmas. Italian stores will usually not give refunds, so be sure you are satisfied with what you purchase.

It is wise to observe shopping etiquette in smaller stores. It is polite to ask to be shown something, unlike in North America where we simply help ourselves. Most shops have cash registers and give printed receipts. If you don't see a cash register - haggle; it usually means the price is flexible.

Most shops are open from 9:00 or 9:30 a.m. to 7:00 or 8:00 p.m. and are closed from 1:00 - 4:00 p.m. for lunch. However, working hours may vary from region to region and with the seasons. Most shops are closed on Monday, except perhaps in resort areas. During summer vacation, not all stores in major cities and towns are open.

SIGN LANGUAGE

ENTRATA	ENTRANCE
USCITA	EXIT
CHIUSO	CLOSED
USCITA DI EMERGENZA	EMERGENCY EXIT
ORARIO...	OPEN FROM...TO...
SPINGERE	PUSH
TIRARE	PULL

SIGN LANGUAGE

In store windows...

SVENDITA	SALE
SALDI DI FINE DI STAGIONE	END-OF-SEASON SALE
LIQUIDAZIONE or VENDITA TOTALE	LIQUIDATION SALE
PREZZI FISSI	FIXED PRICES

Other signs you'll see...

ALIMENTARI	ah-lee-mehn-**tah**-ree	GROCERY STORE
ANTIQUARIO	ahn-tee-**kwah**-ree-oh	ANTIQUE STORE
CALZATURE	kahl-tsah-**too**-reh	FOOTWEAR
CANTINA	kahn-**tee**-nah	WINE MERCHANT
DISCHI	**dee**-skee	MUSIC
EDICOLA/ GIORNALAIO	eh-**dee**-koh-lah/ jyohr-nah-**lah**-yoh	NEWSSTAND
ENOTECA	eh-noh-**teh**-kah	LIQUOR STORE
FARMACIA	fahr-mah-**chee**-ah	PHARMACY
FOTO-OTTICA	foh-toh-**oht**-tee-kah	CAMERA SHOP
GIOIELLERIA	jyoh-yehl-leh-**ree**-ah	JEWELRY
IL GRANDE MAGAZZINO	eel **grahn**-deh mah-gah-**dzee**-noh	DEPARTMENT STORE
LIBRERIA	lee-breh-**ree**-ah	BOOKSTORE
MACELLERIA	mah-chehl-leh-**ree**-ah	BUTCHER
MERCATO	mehr-**kah**-toh	MARKET
MOBILI	**moh**-bee-lee	FURNITURE
PANIFICIO	pahn-nee-**fee**-chyoh	BAKERY
PELLETTERIA	pehl-leh-teh-**ree**-ah	LEATHER GOODS
PROFUMERIA	proh-foo-meh-**ree**-ah	COSMETICS
REGALI (SOUVENIR)	reh-**gah**-lee	GIFT SHOP
SALE E TABACCHI	**sah**-leh eh tah-**bak**-kee	VARIETY STORE
SALUMERIA	sah-loo-meh-**ree**-ah	DELICATESSEN
SUPERMERCATO	soo-pehr-mehr-**kah**-toh	SUPERMARKET
TABACCHERIA	tah-bahk-keh-**ree**-ah	TOBACCO

BEING SERVED

Can you help me?	Mi può aiutare?	mee **pwoh** ah-yoo-**tah**-reh
Where can I find...?	*Dov'è si trove...?*	*dohv-**eh** see **troh**-vah*
Can you show me...?	*Può mostrarmi...?*	*pwoh mohs-trahr-mee*
this	questo	**kweh**-stoh
that	quello	**kwehl**-loh
the one in the window	quello in vetrina	**kwehl**-loh een veh-**tree**-nah
something better	qualcosa di migliore	kwahl-**koh**-zah dee mee-**lyoh**-reh
something less expensive	qualcosa di meno caro	kwahl-**koh**-zah dee **meh**-noh **kah**-roh
a different color	un colore diverso	oon koh-**loh**-reh dee-**vehr**-soh
a different style	un modello diverso	oon moh-**dehl**-loh dee-**vehr**-soh
I would like something for (my)...	*Vorrei qualcosa per...*	*vohr-**ray** kwahl-**koh**-zah pehr*
husband	mio marito	**mee**-oh mah-**ree**-toh
wife	mia moglie	**mee**-ah **moh**-lyeh
son	mio figlio	**mee**-oh **fee**-lyoh
daughter	mia figlia	**mee**-ah **fee**-lyah
for a girl of eight	una ragazza di otto anni	**oo**-nah rah-**gah**-tsah dee **oht**-toh **ahn**-nee
for a boy of 15	un ragazzo di quindici anni	oon rah-**gah**-tsoh dee **kween**-dee-chee **ahn**-nee
Can I try it on?	Lo posso provare?	loh **pohs**-soh proh-**vah**-reh
Do you have a mirror?	Ha uno specchio?	ah **oo**-noh **spek**-kyoh
How much does this cost?	Quanto costa questo?	**kwahn**-toh **koh**-stah **kweh**-stoh
Can I pay...?	*Posso pagare...?*	***pohs**-soh pah-**gah**-reh*
in dollars	in dollari	een **dohl**-lah-ree
with traveller's cheques	con traveller's cheques	kohn traveller's cheques
with a credit card	con la carta di credito	kohn lah **kahr**-tah dee **kreh**-dee toh

Do I have to pay the value added tax?	Devo pagare l'IVA?	**deh**-voh pah-**gah**-reh **lee**-vah
Can you give me a discount?	Mi può fare lo sconto?	mee **pwoh fah**-reh loh **skohn**-toh
It's a gift. Can you wrap it?	È un regalo. Me lo può incartare?	eh oon reh-**gah**-loh meh loh **pwoh** een-karh-tah-reh

DECISIONS

Can you...?	*Me lo può...?*	*meh loh **pwoh***
order it	ordinare	ohr-dee-**nah**-reh
send it	spedire	speh-**dee**-reh
deliver to this address	far recapitare a questo indirizzo	fahr reh-kah-pee-**tah**-reh ah **kweh**-stoh een-dee-**ree**-tsoh
This is damaged.	È rovinato.	eh roh-vee-**nah**-toh
Do you have another one?	Ne ha un altro?	neh ah oon **ahl**-troh
It's very expensive.	È molto caro.	eh **mohl**-toh **kah**-roh
I will (won't) take this.	(Non) lo prendo.	(nohn) loh **prehn**-doh
I'm just looking.	Do solo un'occhiata.	doh **soh**-loh oon ohk-**kyah**-tah
I'll think about it.	Ci penserò.	chee pehn-seh-**roh**
I'm waiting for my wife / husband.	Sto aspettando mia moglie / mio marito.	stoh ah-speh-**tahn**-doh **mee**-ah **moh**-lyeh/ **mee**-oh mah-**ree**-toh
Sorry. I'll look somewhere else.	Mi dispiace. Cercherò da un'altra parte.	mee dee-**spyah**-cheh chehr-keh-**roh** dah oon **ahl**-trah **pahr**-teh
Can I exchange this?	Lo posso cambiare?	loh **pohs**-soh kahm-**byah**-reh
Here is the receipt.	Ecco la ricevuta.	**ehk**-koh lah ree-cheh-**voo**-tah
I'd like my money back.	Vorrei in dietro i soldi.	vohr-**ray** een dee-**eh**-troh ee **sohl**-dee
That will be all.	È tutto.	eh **toot**-toh
(No), thank you!	(No) grazie!	(noh) **grah**-tsyeh

What you may hear

Buon giorno / Buona sera!	bwohn **jyohr**-noh / **bwoh**-nah **seh**-rah	Good morning / Good evening.
Si accomodi / Prego.	see ahk-**koh**-moh-dee / **preh**-goh	Please come in.
Desidera?	deh-**zee**-deh-rah	What would you like?
Mi dica?	mee **dee**-kah	May I help you?
Che misura?	keh mee-**zoo**-rah	What size?
Che numero porta?	keh **noo**-meh-roh **pohr**-tah	What size (shoes)?
Che colore?	keh koh-**loh**-reh	What color?
Le sta bene.	lay stah **beh**-neh	It suits you very well.
È esaurito.	eh eh-zah-oo-**ree**-toh	It's out of stock.
Non ne abbiamo più grande (piccolo).	nohn neh ahb-**byah**-moh pyoo **grahn**-deh (**peek**-koh-loh)	We don't have anything larger (smaller).
Grazie e arrivederLa. (Formal)	**grah**-tsyeh eh ahr-ree-veh-**dehr**-lah	Thank you. Goodbye.

MINI-DICTIONARY

CLOTHING

I would like to buy a (an)...	*Vorrei comperare*	*vohr-**ray** kohm-peh-**rah**-reh*
bathing suit	un costume di bagno	oon koh-**stoo**-meh dee **bah**-nyoh
bathrobe	un accappatoio	oon ahk-kah-pah-**toh**-yoh
belt	una cintura	**oo**-nah cheen-**too**-rah
blouse	una camicetta	**oo**-nah kah-mee-**cheht**-tah
boots	un paio di stivali	oon **pah**-yoh dee stee-**vah**-lee
brassiere	un reggiseno	oon reh-jee-**seh**-noh
coat	un cappotto	onn kahp-**poht**-toh
dress	un vestito	oon veh-**stee**-toh
evening dress	un abito da sera	oon **ah**-bee-toh dah **seh**-rah
fur coat	una pelliccia	**oo**-nah pehl-**lee**-chyah
gloves	dei guanti	**deh**-ee **gwahn**-tee

I would like to buy a (an)...	*Vorrei comperare*	*vohr-**ray** kohm-peh-**rah**-reh*
handbag	una borsetta	**oo**-nah bohr-**seht**-tah
hat	un cappello	oon kah-**pehl**-loh
jacket	una giacca	**oo**-nah **jyahk**-kah
jeans	dei jeans	**deh**-ee jeans
panties	delle mutandine	**dehl**-leh moo-tahn-**dee**-neh
pants	dei pantaloni	**deh**-ee pahn-tah-**loh**-nee
pantyhose	dei collant	**deh**-ee kohl-**lahnt**
raincoat	un impermeabile	oon eem-pehr-mee-**ah**-bee-leh
scarf	una sciarpa	**oo**-nah **shyahr**-pah
shirt	una camicia	**oo**-nah kah-**mee**-chyah
shoes	un paio di scarpe	oon **pah**-yoh dee **skahr**-peh
shorts (men's)	dei pantaloni corti	**deh**-ee pahn-tah-**loh**-nee **kohr**-tee
skirt	una gonna	**oo**-nah **gohn**-nah
socks	dei calzini	**deh**-ee kahl-**tzee**-nee
sports jacket	una giacca sportiva	**oo**-nah **jyahk**-kah spohr-**tee**-vah
suit (man's)	un abito	oon **ah**-bee-toh
suit (woman's)	un tailleur	oon tah-**yehr**
sweater	un maglione	oon mah-**lyoh**-neh
sweatshirt	una felpa	**oo**-nah **fehl**-pah
T-shirt	una maglietta	**oo**-nah mah-**lyeht**-tah
tie	una cravatta	oo-nah krah-**vaht**-tah
turtleneck sweater	un maglione con collo alto	oon mah-**lyoh**-neh kohn **kohl**-loh **ahl**-toh
umbrella	un ombrello	oon ohm-**brehl**-loh
underwear	delle mutande	**dehl**-leh moo-**tahn**-deh
vest	un gilet	oon zhee-**leh**

Shoes

I'd like to see the shoes (boots) in the window.	Vorrei vedere il paio di scarpe (stivali) in vetrina.	vohr-**ray** oon **pah**-yoh dee **skahr**-peh (stee-**vah**-lee) een veh-**tree**-nah
I don't know my size.	Non so il numero.	nohn soh eel **noo**-meh-roh
They're too narrow/wide.	Sono troppo stretti/ larghe.	**soh**-noh **trohp**-poh **streht**-tee (**lahr**-gheh)
They pinch (are too tight).	Mi stanno stretti.	mee **stahn**-noh **trohp**-poh **streht**-tee
They fit well.	Mi stanno bene.	mee **stahn**-noh **beh**-neh
Do yo have a larger/ smaller size?	Ha un numero più grande/piccolo?	ah oon **noo**-meh-roh py**oo** **grahn**-deh/**pee**-koh-loh
I'd like the same one in black.	Vorrei le stesse in nero.	vohr-**ray** leh **stehs**-seh een **neh**-roh
I'll take them.	Le compro.	leh **kohm**-proh

Size

I don't know my size.	Non so la mia taglia.	nohn soh lah **mee**-ah **tah**-lyah
Can I try it on?	Dove posso provarlo?	**doh**-veh **pohs**-soh proh-**vahr**-loh
Do you have a mirror?	C'è uno specchio?	cheh **oo**-noh **spehk**-kyoh
It fits well.	Mi sta bene.	mee stah **beh**-neh
It doesn't fit.	Non mi sta bene.	nohn mee stah **beh**-neh
It's too...	*É troppo...*	*eh **trohp**-poh*
short	corto	**kohr**-toh
long	lungo	**loon**-goh
narrow/tight	stretto	**streht**-toh
wide/large	largo/grande	**lahr**-goh/**grahn**-deh
Can you alter it?	Può aggiustarmelo?	**pwoh** ah-jyoo-**stahr**-meh-loh
When will it be ready?	Quando sarà pronto?	**kwahn**-doh **sah**-rah **prohn**-toh
If I change my mind, can I return the article?	Se non mi va, posso portarlo in dietro?	seh nohn mee vah, **pohs**-soh pohr-**tahr**-loh een **dyeh**-troh

Color

I would like something in...	*Vorrei (qualcosa) in...*	*vohr-**ray** (kwahl-**koh**-zah) een*
beige	beige	behzh
black	nero	**neh**-roh
blue	blu	**bloo**
brown	marrone	mahr-**roh**-neh
green	verde	**vehr**-deh
grey	grigio	**gree**-jyoh
orange	arancione	ah-rahn-**chyoh**-neh
pink	rosa	**roh**-zah
red	rosso	**rohs**-soh
purple	viola	vee-**oh**-lah
white	bianco	**byahn**-koh
yellow	giallo	**jyahl**-loh
lighter	più chiaro	pyoo **kyah**-roh
darker	più scuro	pyoo **skoo**-roh
in a solid color	in tinta unita	een **teen**-tah oo-**nee**-tah
with stripes	a righe	ah **ree**-gheh
with polka dots	a pois	ah pwoh
in plaid	di scozzese	dee skoh-**tseh**-zeh
checked	a scacchi	ah **skah**-kee

Color adjectives that end in o agree in number and gender with the noun they modify. The o is changed to an a with nouns that are feminine, for example, un cappello rosso—una sciarpa rossa. **Arancione**, **blu**, **marrone**, **rosa**, **viola** do not change; for example, un cappotto marrone.

Material

I'd prefer something in...	*Preferisco qualcosa in...*	*preh-feh-**ree**-skoh kwahl-**koh**-zah een*
corduroy	velluto a coste	vehl-**loo**-toh ah **koh**-steh
cotton	cotone	koh-**toh**-neh
denim	tela	**teh**-lah
gabardine	gabardine	gah-bahr-**deen**
lace	pizzo	**pee**-tsoh
leather	pelle	**pehl**-leh
linen	lino	**lee**-noh
satin	raso	**rah**-zoh
silk	seta	**seh**-tah
suede	camoscio	kah-**moh**-shyoh
synthetic	poliestere	poh-**lyeh**-streh
terry cloth	spugna	**spoo**-nyah
velvet	velluto	vehl-**loo**-toh
wool	lana	**lah**-nah

Conversion Chart for Clothing and Shoe Sizes

Women's shoes

Canadian	6	7	8	8.5	9
Italian	36	37	38	38.5	40

Women's dresses and suits

Canadian	6	8	10	12	14	16	18
Italian	38	40	42	44	46	48	50

Men's suits and overcoats

Canadian	36	38	40	42	44	46
Italian	46	48	50	52	54	56

Men's shirts

Canadian	15	16	17	18
Italian	38	41	43	45

Men's shoes

Canadian	7	8	8.5	9	9 1/2	10	11
Italian	39	41	42	42.5	43	44	44.5

SOUVENIRS, HANDICRAFTS

I'd like...	*Vorrei...*	*vohr-**ray***
a nice gift	un bel regalo	oon behl reh-**gah**-loh
a small gift	un regalino	oon reh-gah-**lee**-noh
a souvenir	un souvenir	oon souvenir
I'm looking for...	*Cerco...*	***chehr**-koh*
blown glass	il vetro soffiato	eel **veh**-troh soh-**fyah**-toh
carved wood	il legno intagliato	eel **leh**-nyoh een-tah-**lyah**-toh
crystal	il cristallo	eel kree-**stahl**-loh
pottery	le ceramiche	leh cheh-**rah**-mee-keh
jewelry	gli oggetti preziosi	lyee oh-**jeht**-tee preh-**tsyoh**-zee
lace	i pizzi	ee **pee**-tsee
leather goods	gli articoli in pelle	lyee ahr-**tee**-koh-lee een **pehl**-leh
liqueurs	i liquori	ee lee-**kwoh**-ree
perfumes	i profumi	ee proh-**foo**-mee
a poster	un poster	oon **poh**-stehr
religious articles	gli articoli religiosi	lyee ahr-**tee**-koh-lee reh-lee-**jyoh**-zee
local handicrafts	i prodotti dell'artigianato locale	ee proh-**doht**-tee dehl ahr-tee-jyah-**nah**-toh loh-**kah**-leh

NEWSSTAND

I'm looking for a newsstand.	Cerco un'edicola.	**chehr**-koh oon eh-**dee**-koh-lah
I would like, please...	*Vorrei...*	*vohr-**ray***
a newspaper in English	una rivista in inglese	**oo**-nah ree-**vee**-stah een een-**gleh**-zeh
a map of the city	una pianta della città	oo-nah **pyahn**-tah **dehl**-lah cheet-**tah**
postcards	delle cartoline	**dehl**-leh kahr-toh-**lee**-neh
stamps	dei francobolli	**deh**-ee frahn-koh-**bohl**-lee

STATIONERY STORE

I'm looking for a stationery store.	Cerco una cartoleria.	**chehr**-koh **oo**-nah kahr-toh-leh-**ree**-ah
I would like...	*Vorrei...*	*vohr-**ray***
a pen	una penna	**oo**-nah **pehn**-nah
some envelopes	delle buste	**dehl**-leh **boo**-steh
a notebook	un quaderno	oon kwah-**dehr**-noh
stationery	della carta da lettere	**dehl**-lah **kahr**-tah dah **leht**-teh-reh

CAMERA SHOP

Where is a camera shop?	Dov'è un negozio di foto-ottica?	dohv-**eh** oon neh-**goh**-tsyoh dee foh-toh-**oht**-tee-kah
I want a (an)...	*Voglio...*	***voh**-lyoh*
battery	una pila.	**oo**-nah **pee**-lah
color/black and white film	una pellicola a colori (in bianco e nero)	**oo**-nah pehl-**lee**-koh-lah ah koh-**loh**-ree (een **byahn**-koh eh **neh**-roh)
print film	una pellicola per stampe	**oo**-nah pehl-**lee**-koh-lah pehr **stahm**-peh
film for slides	una pellicola per diapositive	**oo**-nah pehl-**lee**-koh-lah pehr dee-ah-poh-zee-**tee**-vee
video film	un video	oon **vee**-deh-oh
May I have this developed?	Sviluppano i rullini?	svee-**loo**-pah-noh ee rool-**lee**-nee
How much does it cost?	Quanto costa far sviluppare il film?	**kwahn**-toh **koh**-stah fahr svee-loo-**pah**-reh eel feelm
One (two) prints of each.	Una copia (due copie).	**oo**-nah **koh**-pee-ah (**doo**-eh **koh**-pee-eh)
When will it be ready?	Quando vengo a ritirarli?	**kwahn**-doh **vehn**-goh ah ree-tee-**rahr**-lee

TOBACCO SHOP

Look for a small blue sign that reads **Sale e Tabacchi**. In addition to cigarettes, they also sell candy, small toys, cards and stamps.

I'm looking for a cigarette shop.	Cerco una tabaccheria.	**chehr**-koh **oo**-nah tah-bahk-keh-**ree**-ah
I would like a package (carton) of...	*Vorrei un pacchetto (una stecca)...*	*vohr-**ray** oon pahk-**keht**-toh (**oo**-nah **stehk**-kah)*
filtered	con filtro	kohn **feel**-troh
non-filtered	senza filtro	**sehn**-zah **feel**-troh
menthol	alla menta	**ahl**-lah **mehn**-teh
king-size	lunghe	**loon**-ghe
American cigarettes	delle sigarette americane	**dehl**-leh see-gah-**reht**-teh ah-meh-ree-**kah**-neh
I would like...	*Vorrei...*	*vohr-**ray***
a cigar	un sigaro	oon see-**gah**-roh
lighter	l'accendino	lah-chehn-**dee**-noh
matches	una scatola di fiammiferi	**oo**-nah **skah**-toh-lah dee fyah-**mee**-feh-ree
Are these cigarettes (very) strong (mild)?	Sono (molto) forti (leggere) queste sigarette?	**soh**-noh (**mohl**-toh) fohr-tee (leh-**jeh**-reh) **kweh**-steh see-gah-**reht**-teh

TOILETRIES

Toiletries and perfumes are available at major department stores and at the **Profumeria**. See chapter 12 for a more extensive list of pharmaceutical needs.

I would like a (an)...	*Vorrei...*	*vohr-**ray***
brush	una spazzola	**oo**-nah **spah**-tsoh-lah
cleansing cream	la crema detergente	lah **kreh**-mah deh-tehr-**jehn**-teh
comb	un pettine	oon **peht**-tee-neh
condoms	dei preservativi	**deh**-ee preh-sehr-vah-**tee**-vee
deodorant	un deodorante	oon deh-oh-doh-**rahn**-teh

diapers	dei pannolini per bambini	**deh**-ee pahn-noh-**lee**-nee pehr bahm-**bee**-nee
razor blades	delle lamette	**dehl**-leh lah-**meht**-teh
razor	un rasoio	oon rah-**zoh**-yoh
sanitary napkins	degli assorbenti igienici	**deh**-lyee ahs-sohr-**behn**-tee ee-**jeh**-nee-chee
scissors	delle forbici	**dehl**-leh **fohr**-bee-chee
shampoo	dello shampoo	**dehl**-loh **shahm**-poo
shaving lotion	un dopobarba	oon doh-poh-**bahr**-bah
soap	del sapone	dehl sah-**poh**-neh
suntan lotion	una crema solare	**oo**-nah **kreh**-mah soh-**lah**-reh
tampons	dei tamponi	**deh**-ee tahm-**poh**-nee
toothbrush	uno spazzolino da denti	**oo**-noh spah-tsoh-**lee**-noh dah **dehn**-tee
toothpaste	del dentifricio	dehl dehn-tee-**free**-chyoh

BOOKSTORE

I'm looking for a bookstore.	Cerco una libreria.	**chehr**-koh **oo**-nah lee-breh-**ree**-ah
I'd like this guide book in English.	Vorrei questa guida in inglese.	vohr-**ray** **kweh**-stah **gwee**-dah een een-**gleh**-zeh
I need a (an)...	*Ho bisogno di...*	*oh bee-**zoh**-nyoh dee*
city map	una pianta della città	**oo**-nah **pyahn**-tah **dehl**-lah **cheet**-tah
English-Italian dictionary	un dizionario italiano-inglese	oon dee-tsyoh-**nah**-ree-oh ee-tah-**lyah**-noh-een-**gleh**-zeh
pocket dictionary	un dizionario tascabile	oon dee-tsyoh-**nah**-ree-oh tah-**skah**-bee-leh
road map	una carta stradale	**oo**-nah **kahr**-tah strah-**dah**-leh
travel guide	una guida turistica	**oo**-nah **gwee**-dah too-**ree**-stee-kah

MUSIC

Is there a music store nearby?	C'è un negozio di musica qui vicino?	cheh oon neh-**goh**-tsyoh dee **moo**-zee-kah kwee vee-**chee**-noh
I'd like to buy...	*Vorrei comprare...*	*vohr-**ray** kohm-**prah**-reh*
cassettes	delle cassette	**deh**-leh kahs-**seht**-teh
CDs	dei ciddi	**deh**-ee chee-**dee**
tapes	dei nastri	**deh**-ee **nah**-stree
Where is the...section?	*Dov'è la sezione...?*	*dohv-**eh** lah seh-**tsyoh**-neh*
classical music	di musica classica	dee **moo**-zee-kah **klahs**-see-kah
opera	musica d'opera	**moo**-zee-kah **doh**-peh-rah
popular songs and music	di musica popolare	dee **moo**-zee-kah poh-poh-**lah**-reh
latest hits	degli ultimi successi	**deh**-lyee **ool**-tee-mee soo-**chehs**-see
Italian music	della musica italiana	**dehl**-lah **moo**-zee-kah ee-tah-**lyah**-nah
May I listen to it?	Posso ascoltarlo?	**pohs**-soh ah-skohl-**tahr**-loh?
Good, I'll take it.	Va bene. Lo prendo.	vah **beh**-neh. loh **prehn**-doh

GROCERY SHOPPING

Pick up a bottle of wine, some cheese, sliced meat and bread for a quick lunch or dinner at the beach or on the road. Use either of the first two phrases to help find what you need.

Where (is) can I find...?	*Dove si trova...?*	***doh**-veh see **troh**-vah*
I would like a (an)...	*Vorrei...*	*vohr-**ray***
bottle of juice	un succo di frutta	oon **sook**-koh dee **froot**-tah
bottle of mineral water	una bottiglia d' acqua minerale	**oo**-nah boht-**tee**-lyah **dah**-kwah mee-neh-**rah**-leh

dozen eggs	una dozzina di uova	**oo**-nah doh-**dzee**-nah dee **woh**-vah
100 grams of cheese	cento grammi di formaggio	**chehn**-toh **grahm**-mee dee fohr-**mah**-jyoh
package of candies	un pacchetto di caramelle	oon pah-**keht**-toh dee kah-rah-**mehl**-leh
box of chocolates	una scatola di cioccolatini	**oo**-nah **skah**-toh-lah **deh**-ee chyoh-koh-lah-**tee**-nee
six cans of coke	sei lattine di coca	**seh**-ee laht-**tee**-neh dee **koh**-kah
cake	una torta	**oo**-nah **tohr**-tah
litre of milk	un litro di latte	oon **lee**-troh dee **laht**-teh
bottle of wine	una bottiglia di vino	**oo**-nah boht-**tee**-lyah dee **vee**-noh
100 grams of mortadella	cento grammi (un etto) di mortadella	**chehn**-toh **grahm**-mee (oon **eht**-toh) dee mohr-tah-**dehl**-lah
I would also like some bread	Vorrei anche dei panini.	Vohr-**ray** **ahn**-keh **deh**-ee pah-**nee**-nee

CHAPTER NINE

Sightseeing

While walking around any Italian city, be aware of the street signs. Italian drivers have no compunction about showing their displeasure with pedestrians who get in their way. They may just blow their horn but often they will have something to say to you. Be especially vigilant when crossing on a one-way street. You had better be looking in the right direction! If you decide that a picture must be taken from the middle of a **circonvallazione** (traffic circle, round-about), you may get there easily enough, but when the traffic signals change or the **carabinieri** blows his whistle, you may be stuck there for quite a while. Arrange for your travel companions to take a picture of you, and then meet them in the nearest **osteria**, **gelateria** or **bar** (same word in Italian!).

SIGN LANGUAGE

ALT! STOP!	STOP!
ATTENZIONE!	CAUTION/DANGER!
AUTOBUS	BUS STOP
AVANTI	GO!
CENTRO CITTÀ	TO THE CENTER OF TOWN
FERMATA DEI TAXI	TAXI STAND
FILOBUS	TROLLEYBUS STOP
METROPOLITANA	METRO
PASSAGGIO PEDONALE	PEDESTRIAN CROSSING
PERICOLO!	DANGER!
SENSO UNICO	ONE-WAY TRAFFIC
TAXI	TAXI

SIGHTSEEING

In your walks in the cities, you may often stop and ask directions. Asking the question **Where (is)...? - Dov'è...?** or **How do you get to...? - Per andare a...?** will usually get you a long and incomprehensible answer! For such questions, the Italian phrases below will help you and your listener with directions.

Where (is)...?	Dov'è...?	dohv-**eh**
How do you get to...?	Per andare a...?	pehr ahn-**dah**-reh ah
I'm lost.	Mi sono perso (-a).	mee **soh**-noh **pehr**-soh
Please point it out.	Per favore me lo mostri?	pehr fah-**voh**-reh meh loh **mohs**-tree

What you may hear

Bisogna prendere...	*bee-**zoh**-nyah **prehn**-deh-reh*	*Take...*
l'autobus numero...	**low**-toh-boos **noo**-meh-roh	bus number...
la metropolitana	lah meh-troh-poh-lee-**tah**-nah	the metro
un taxi	oon tahk-**see**	a taxi
Ha sbagliato la strada.	ah zbah-**lyah**-toh lah **stah**-dah	You're not going in the right direction.
Ci si può andare a piedi.	chee see **pwoh** ahn-**dah**-reh ah-**pyeh**-dee	You can walk there.
Non ci si può andare a piedi.	nohn chee see **pwoh** ahn-**dah**-reh ah **pyeh**-dee	You can't walk there.
È...	***eh***	*It's...*
a sinistra	ah see-**nee**-strah	to the left
a destra	ah **deh**-strah	to the right
accanto a	ahk-**kahn**-toh ah	next to
al di là della strada	ahl dee lah **dehl**-lah **strah**-dah	on the other side of the street
all'angolo	ahl-**ahn**-goh-loh	on the corner
all'incrocio	ahl-een-**kroh**-chyoh	at the intersection
davanti a	dah-**vahn**-tee ah	in front of
in dietro	een **dyeh**-troh	back

È...	***eh***	*It's...*
dopo	**doh**-poh	after
dopo il semaforo	**doh**-poh eel seh-**mah**-foh-roh	after the traffic light
circa dieci minuti a piedi (in macchina)	**cheer**-kah **dyeh**-chee mee-**noo**-tee ah **pyeh**-dee (een **mahk**-kee-nah)	approximately 10 minutes walking (driving)
sempre diritto	**sehm**-preh dee-**reet**-toh	straight ahead
là	**lah**	there
vicino	vee-**chee**-noh	nearby (close)
lontano	lohn-**tah**-noh	far
Non so.	nohn **soh**	I don't know.
L'accompagno.	lahk-kohm-**pah**-nyoh	I'll show you the way.

TOUR GUIDES

If you are not with a tour group, you may wish to hire your own guide for a day to do a quick overview of the city. Be sure to get a firm quote for the entire cost.

Where is the tourist information office?	Dov'è l'Ente Locale (Nazionale) per il Turismo?	dohv-**eh lehn**-teh loh-**kah**-leh (nah-tsyoh-**nah**-leh) pehr eel too-**reez**-moh
Are there tours of the city?	Si fanno dei tour della città?	see **fahn**-noh deh-ee toor **deh**-lah cheet-**tah**
Where can I buy an English guide book?	Dove posso comprare una guida turistica in inglese?	**doh**-veh **pohs**-soh kohm-**prah**-reh **oo**-nah **gwee**-dah too-**ree**-stee-kah een een-**gleh**-zeh
I need an English-speaking guide.	Ho bisogno di una guida che parla inglese.	oh bee-**soh**-nyoh dee **oo**-nah **gwee**-dah keh **pahr**-lah een-**gleh**-zeh
How much...?	*Quanto si fa pagare...?*	***kwahn**-toh see fah pah-**gah**-reh*
per hour	all'ora	ahl-**oh**-rah
for the day	al giorno	ahl **jyohr**-noh
We would like to see the city.	Vogliamo vedere la città.	voh-**lyah**-moh veh-**deh**-reh lah cheet-**tah**

When does the tour leave?	Quando inizia il tour?	**kwahn**-doh ee-**nee**-tsyah eel toor
How long is the tour?	Quanto dura il tour?	**kwahn**-toh **doo**-rah eel toor
There are two (four, six) of us.	Siamo in due (quattro, sei).	see-**ah**-moh een **doo**-eh (**kwaht**-troh, **seh**-ee)
Where does the tour start?	Da dove iniziano i tour?	dah **doh**-veh een-**nee**-tsyah-noh ee toor?
When do we return to the hotel?	A che ora si ritorna in albergo?	ah keh **oh**-rah see ree-**tohr**-nah een ahl-**behr**-goh?

MINI-DICTIONARY

We would like to see...	*Vogliamo vedere...*	*voh-lyee-**ah**-moh veh-**deh**-reh*
What is this....called?	*Come si chiama?... (questo) (quello)*	***koh**-meh see **kyah**-mah **kweh**-stoh*
abbey	l'abbazia	lahb-**bah**-tsyah
art gallery	la galleria d'arte	lah gahl-leh-**ree**-ah **dahr**-teh
botanical gardens	il giardino botanico	eel jyarh-**dee**-noh boh-**tah**-nee-koh
business center	il centro commerciale	eel **chehn**-troh kohm-mehr-**chyah**-leh
castle	il castello	eel kah-**stehl**-loh
catacomb	le catacombe	kah-tah-**kohm**-beh
cathedral	la cattedrale	lah kaht-teh-**drah**-leh
caves	le grotte	leh **groht**-teh
church	la chiesa	lah **kyeh**-zah
concert hall	la sala dei concerti	lah **sah**-lah **deh**-ee kohn-**chehr**-tee
convent	il convento	eel kohn-**vehn**-toh
downtown area	la zona del centro	lah **dzoh**-nah del **chehn**-troh
fortress	la fortezza	lah fohr-**teht**-tsah
fountains	le fontane	leh fohn-**tah**-neh
government buildings	il palazzo comunale	eel pah-**laht**-tsoh kohm-moo-**nah**-leh

We would like to see...	*Vogliamo vedere...*	*voh-lyee-**ah**-moh veh-**deh**-reh*
What is this....called?	*Come si chiama?... (questo) (quello)*	***koh**-meh see **kyah**-mah **kweh**-stoh*
harbor	il porto	eel **pohr**-toh
historic sites	i luoghi storici	ee **lwoh**-ghee **stoh**-ree-chee
library	la biblioteca	lah bee-blee-oh-**teh**-kah
main park	la piazza principale	lah pee-**aht**-tsah preen-chee-**pah**-leh
monastery	i monumenti	ee moh-noo-**mehn**-tee
mosque	la moschea	lah mohs-**keh**-ah
museum...	*il museo...*	*eel moo-**zeh**-oo*
of art	delle belle arti	**dehl**-leh **behl**-leh **ahr**-tee
of modern art	d'arte moderna	**dahr**-teh moh-**dehr**-nah
of natural sciences	di scienze naturali	dee shee-**ehn**-zah nah-too-**rah**-lee
opera house	il teatro dell'opera	eel teh-**ah**-troh dehl-**oh**-peh-rah
palace	il palazzo	eel pah-**laht**-tsoh
square	la piazza	lah pee-**aht**-tsah
statue	la statua	lah stah-too-ah
synagogue	la sinagoga	lah see-nah-**goh**-gah
tomb	la tomba	lah **tohm**-bah
university	l'università	loo-nee-vehr-see-**tah**
zoo	lo zoo	loh **dzoh**
Would you take our picture?	Ci fa una foto?	chee fah **oo**-nah **foh**-toh
One more shot.	Ancora una.	ahn-**koh**-rah **oo**-nah
Thank you very much.	Grazie mille.	**grah**-tsyeh **meel**-leh

TAXIS IN THE CITY

Find the taxi stand. Have your address or hotel name written down to show the driver. You will be asked, **Dove andate? (Doh**-veh ahn-**dah**-teh?) – Where do you want to go? The driver may also decline to take you to your destination if it's late and he's decided to go home, or if your destination is too far out of the way to pick up a return fare. If you hire a private car, fix the price before you go.

Taxis are metered, but ask for the price of your trip before you get in. A supplement is usually added after 10:00 p.m. At taxi stands, there is usually a drop-off and pick-up area, where people will line up. In busy times, some will jump the line so "when in Rome..." you may have to "do as the Romans do." Be prepared for grumbling from the locals!

Is there a taxi stand nearby?	C'è un posteggio dei taxi vicino?	cheh oon poh-**steh**-jyoh **deh**-ee tahk-**see** vee-**chee**-noh
Are you free (taxi)?	È libero?	eh **lee**-beh-roh
Can you take me to the...?	*Mi porti...?*	*mee* ***pohr**-tee*
airport	all'aeroporto	ahl-ah-eh-roh-**pohr**-toh
bus station	alla stazione autolinee	**ahl**-lah stah-**tsyoh**-neh ow-toh-**lee**-neh-eh
city center	in centro	een **chehn**-troh
hotel	all'hotel	ahl-oh-**tehl**
main square	alla piazza principale	**ahl**-lah **pyah**-tsah preen-chee-**pah**-leh
(this) restaurant	a questo ristorante	ah **kweh**-stoh ree-stoh-**rahn**-teh
(this) store	a questo negozio	ah **kweh**-stoh neh-**goh**-tsyoh
street	in via...	een **vee**-ah
train station	alla stazione	**ahl**-lah stah-**tsyoh**-neh
Do you know where it is?	Sa dove si trova?	sah **doh**-veh see **troh**-vah
How much for...?	Quant'è per...?	kwahnt-**eh** pehr
I'm in a hurry.	Ho fretta.	oh **freht**-tah
Slow down!	Guidi più adagio!	**gwee**-dee pyoo ah-**dah**-jyoh
Stop here!	Si fermi qui!	see **fehr**-mee kwee
Wait for me here. I'll be right back.	Mi aspetti qui. Torno subito.	mee ah-**speht**-tee kwee **tohr**-noh **soo**-bee-toh

I think you are going the wrong way.	Penso che lei abbia sbagliato la strada.	**pehn**-soh keh **leh**-ee ahb-byah sbah-**lyah**-toh lah **strah**-dah
How much do I owe you?	Quanto le devo?	**kwahn**-toh leh **deh**-voh
Keep the change.	Tenga il resto.	**tehn**-gah eel **reh**-stoh
This is for you.	Questo è per lei.	**kweh**-stoh eh pehr **leh**-ee
I'll only pay what's on the meter.	Pago solo la cifra sul tassametro.	**pah**-goh **soh**-loh lah **chee**-frah sool tahs-sah-**meh**-troh

Be sure you understand your driver's response. In case of a misunderstanding, note the driver's number.

What you may hear

Si è libero.	see eh **lee**-behr-roh	Yes, I'm free.
Dove andate?	doh-**veh** ahn-**dah**-teh	Where do you want to go?
È occupato.	eh ohk-koo-**pah**-toh	I'm not free.
Vi aspetto qui.	vee ah-**speht**-toh kwee	I'll wait for you.
Non vi posso aspettare.	nohn vee p**ohs**-soh ah-speht-**tah**-reh	I can't wait for you.
Tornerò.	tohr-neh-**roh**	I'll come back for you.
Un momento per favore.	oon moh-**mehn**-toh pehr fah-**voh**-reh	Wait, please.
Non so dove si trova.	nohn soh **doh**-veh see **troh**-vah	I don't know where that is.
La tariffa è cinquantamila lire.	Lah tahr-**reef**-fah eh cheen-**kwahn**-tah-**mee**-lah **lee**-reh	You owe 50.000 lire.
Non ho da cambiare.	Nohn oh dah kahm-**byah**-reh	I don't have change.

In general, people are always willing to help a tourist. Most will be patient and assist you any way they can. Remember to always ask for help, starting with **Per favore...** (Pehr fah-**voh**-reh...).

BUSES, TRAMS, TROLLEY BUSES

Bus tickets can be purchased at tobacco shops, newsstands and automatic ticket machines in advance. Italian cities have extensive bus systems with complete routes and itineraries posted at all bus stops. Validate your tickets on the bus or at the entrance. Fines are given to those with invalidated tickets, and these are payable immediately to the transit inspector.

Where is the nearest bus stop?	Dov'è la fermata più vicina dell'autobus?	dohv-**eh** lah fehr-**mah**-tah py**oo** vee-**chee**-nah dehl-**ow**-toh-boos
Where is the bus station (terminal)?	Dov'è la stazione autolinee?	dohv-**eh** lah stah-**tsyoh**-neh ow-toh-**lee**-neh-eh
What bus (tram) should I take to go to...?	Quale autobus (tram) per andare a...?	**kwah**-leh **ow**-toh-boos (trahm) pehr ahn-**dah**-reh ah
Do you go to...?	Va a...?	vah ah
Is it far from here?	È lontano da qui?	eh lohn-**tah**-noh dah kwee
How many stops to...?	Quante fermate ci sono prima di...?	**kwahn**-teh fehr-**mah**-teh chee **soh**-noh **pree**-mah dee
Must I change (routes)?	Devo cambiare autobus?	**deh**-voh kahm-**byah**-reh **ow**-toh-boos
Please tell me when I must get off.	Può dirmi dove devo scendere?	pw**oh** **deer**-mee **doh**-veh **deh**-voh **shehn**-deh-reh
I want to get off at...	Voglio scendere a...	**voh**-lyoh **shehn**-deh-reh ah

METRO - METROPOLITANA

Both Milan and Rome have good subway systems called the **metropolitana** (meh-troh-poh-lee-**tah**-nah). In Rome only a few lines have been completed because of the many archaeological finds in their path. Nonetheless, the subway is an efficient and fast way to get around. Station entrances are marked with a large **M** and maps are posted on the trains and at every station. The fare is low and will take you through the entire system. Stations are generally announced, and listen for the signal when the doors are closing.

Where is the closest metro station?	Dov'è la stazione più vicina della metropolitana?	dohv-**eh** lah stah-**tsyoh**-neh pyoo vee-**chee**-nah **dehl**-lah meh-troh-poh-lee-**tah**-nah
How much does it cost?	Quanto costa il biglietto (il gettone)?	**kwahn**-toh **koh**-stah eel bee-**lyeht**-toh (eel jeht-**toh**-neh)
Which route do I take to...?	Quale linea va a...?	**kwah**-leh **lee**-neh-ah vah ah
Does this train go to...?	Questo treno va a...?	**kweh**-stoh **treh**-noh vah ah
Where do I change for...?	Dove devo cambiare treno per...?	**doh**-veh **deh**-voh kahm-**byah**-reh **treh**-noh pehr
What is the next stop?	Qual'è la prossima stazione?	qwal **eh** lah **prohs**-see-mah stah-**tsyoh**-neh
How many more stops?	Quante fermate ancora?	**kwahn**-teh fehr-**mah**-teh ahn-**koh**-rah
Where do I get off?	Dove devo scendere?	**doh**-veh **deh**-voh **shehn**-deh-reh

VISITING POINTS OF INTEREST

When visiting museums, historic and military sites, always ask if taking photographs is permitted. If you are not with a tour group or don't have a guide, you may want to join an English-speaking guide for a tour at a particular site.

Many places will not allow you to carry large bags or cameras with flashes, and you will be asked to check them at the entrance.

Most large cities in Italy have organized tours in English. When visiting museums and other points of interest in the country and smaller towns, you are on your own. Museums are generally open from 9:30 a.m. to 4:00 p.m. on weekdays, 9:30 a.m. to 1:00 p.m. on Sundays and holidays. Mondays, museums are generally closed.

ADMISSION

May one enter?	Si può entrare adesso?	see **pwoh** ehn-**trah**-reh ah-**dehs**-soh
Is it open/closed?	È aperto / chiuso?	eh ah-**pehr**-toh
CLOSED	CHIUSO	kyoo-zoh

How much is the admission fee?	Quanto costa l'ingresso?	**kwahn**-toh **koh**-stah leen-**grehs**-soh
Is there a discount for...?	*Fate sconto per...?*	***fah**-teh **skohn**-toh pehr*
youth	giovani	**jyoh**-vah-nee
students	studenti	stoo-**dehn**-tee
children	bambini	bahm-**bee**-nee
seniors	pensionati	pehn-syoh-**nah**-tee
Can I get back in?	Posso rientrare?	**pohs**-soh ree-ehn-**trah**-reh
Please let me in.	Per favore, mi faccia entrare.	pehr fah-**voh**-reh, mee **fah**-chyah ehn-**trah**-reh

SIGN LANGUAGE

VIETATO USARE FLASH/ TREPPIEDE	NO FLASH OR TRIPOD
VIETATO FUMARE!	NO SMOKING!
NON TOCCARE!	DON'T TOUCH!

PHOTOGRAPHY

Can we take pictures?	Si possono fare fotografie?	see **pohs**-soh-noh **fah**-reh foh-toh-grah-**fee**-eh
I won't use flash.	Non uso il flash.	noh **oo**-zoh eel flahsh
We would like to have our picture taken.	Ci fa una foto, per favore?	chee fah **oo**-nah **foh**-toh pehr fah-**voh**-reh
One more shot.	Ancora una.	ahn-**koh**-rah **oo**-nah

RELIGIOUS SERVICES

Most churches are open to the public during services or for tours. Visitors should observe the dress code and respect the silence rules. If you wish to attend services, ask at tourist information or at your hotel.

Excuse me!	Chiedo scusa!	**kyeh**-doh **skoo**-zah
I don't speak Italian.	Non parlo italiano.	nohn **pahr**-loh ee-tah-**lyah**-noh
Thank you very much.	Grazie mille.	**grah**-tsyeh **meel**-leh

CHAPTER TEN

Travel by car and train

If you are travelling by car in Italy, be sure your passport, visa and international driver's license are in order and that you have all the required documents for your car rental. Your travel agent is your best source for up-to-date information. If renting a car in Italy, be sure to ask for maps, traffic regulations and road sign explanations. Plan ahead for your stops for gas. Use of seat belts is mandatory.

On the **Autostrada**, be aware that the passing lane is exactly that. Always look in the rear-view mirror for oncoming flashing lights. That vehicle is intent on passing you, so get out of the way! Also be wary of truck drivers. Their speedometers are locked at 90 kilometres per hour and when they decide to pass, it will take some patience on your part.

On highways and in cities, lanes are usually marked, but don't expect Italian drivers to keep to their lanes. In the cities especially, where there are two lanes, drivers will try to use three and a half! Watch all sides of your car.

On highways and country roads, there is usually a white line to the right on the shoulder. Italian drivers in slow cars or trucks will pull over onto this shoulder area to let you pass. They expect you to do the same!

SIGN LANGUAGE

AUTOSTRADA	TOLL HIGHWAY
CAMPEGGIO	CAMPING (CAMPGROUNDS)
CASELLO	TOLL BOOTH
CIRCONVALLAZIONE	TRAFFIC CIRCLE
CUNETTA (or) DOSSO	BUMPS
CURVE PERICOLOSE	DANGEROUS CURVES
DARE LA PRECEDENZA	YIELD
DEVIAZIONE	DETOUR
DIVIETO DI ACCESSO	NO ENTRY
DIVIETO DI SVOLTA	NO LEFT TURN
	A SINISTRA
DIVIETO DI	NO U-TURN
	INVERSIONE AD "U"
DIVIETO DI SORPASSO	NO PASSING
FINE DIVIETO DI SORPASSO	END OF NO-PASSING ZONE
INCROCIO	INTERSECTION (DANGEROUS)
LAVORI IN CORSO	ROAD CONSTRUCTION
LIMITARE LA VELOCITÀ	REDUCE SPEED
LIMITE DI VELOCITÀ	SPEED LIMIT
PARCHEGGIO	PARKING
PASSAGGIO PEDONALE	PEDESTRIAN CROSSING
PERICOLO	DANGER
SENSO UNICO	ONE WAY TRAFFIC
SOSTA VIETATA	NO PARKING
STOP/ALT	STOP
STRADA PRINCIPALE	MAIN ROAD
STRETTOIA	ROAD NARROWS
TRANSITO VIETATO PER AUTOVEICOLI	NO ENTRY FOR MOTOR VEHICLES
USCITA	EXIT
ZONA PEDONALE	PEDESTRIAN ZONE

CAR RENTAL

Where can I rent a car?	Dove posso noleggiare una macchina?	**doh**-veh **poh**-soh noh-leh-**jyah**-reh **oo**-nah **mahk**-kee-nah
I'd like a (an)...	*Vorrei una macchina...*	*vohr-**ray** **oo**-nah **mahk**-kee-nah*
automatic	col cambio automatico	kohl **kahm**-byoh ow-toh-**mah**-tee-koh
large car	grande	**grahn**-deh
least expensive car	la meno cara	lah **meh**-noh **kah**-rah
small car	piccola	**peek**-koh-lah
station wagon	familiare	fah-mee-**lyah**-reh
I'd like to rent a...	*Vorrei noleggiare...*	*vohr-**ray** noh-leh-**jyah**-reh*
moped	un motorino	oon moh-toh-**ree**-noh
motorcycle	una motocicletta	**oo**-nah moh-toh-chee-**kleht**-tah
How much does it cost...?	*Quanto costa...?*	***kwahn**-toh **koh**-stah*
per day	al giorno	ahl **jyohr**-noh
per week	alla settimana	**ahl**-lah seht-tee-**mah**-nah
per kilometre	per chilometro	pehr kee-**loh**-meh-troh
for unlimited mileage	per chilometraggio illimitato	pehr kee-loh-meh-**trah**-jyoh eel-lee-mee-**tah**-toh
How much is (compete) insurance?	Quant'è l'assicurazione (completa)?	kwahnt-**eh** lahs-see-koo-rah-**tsyoh**-neh (kohm-**pleh**-tah)
Here is my license.	Ecco la mia patente internazionale.	**ehk**-koh lah **mee**-ah pah-**tehn**-teh een-tehr-nah-tsyoh-**nah**-leh
When do I have to return it?	Quando lo riporto in dietro?	**kwahn**-doh loh ree-**pohr**-toh een **dyeh**-troh
Can I leave the car in another city?	Posso lasciare la macchina in un'altra città?	**pohs**-soh lah-**shyah**-reh lah **mahk**-kee-nah een oon **ahl**-troh chee-**tah**

Is there a drop-off charge?	C'è un supplemento per la consegna (dell'auto)?	cheh oon soo-plee-**mehn**-toh pehr lah kohn-**seh**-nyah (dehl-**ow**-toh)
What kind of gasoline does it take?	Che tipo di carburante usa?	keh **tee**-poh dee kahr-boo-**rahn**-teh **oo**-zah
May I have a road map?	Posso avere una carta stradale?	**pohs**-soh ah-**veh**-reh **oo**-nah **kahr**-tah strah-**dah**-leh

PARKING

Take parking restrictions to heart in order avoid getting towed and fined. And leave nothing tempting in your car, especially overnight.

Where can I park?	Dove posso parcheggiare?	**doh**-veh **pohs**-soh pahr-keh-**jyah**-reh
How long can I park here?	Per quanto tempo posso parcheggiare qui?	pehr **kwahn**-toh **tehm**-poh **pohs**-soh pahr-keh-**jyah**-reh kwee
Must I pay to park here?	È a pagamento questo parcheggio?	eh ah pah-gah-**mehn**-toh **kweh**-stoh pahr-**keh**-jyoh
Is this a safe place to park?	È sicuro parcheggiare qui?	eh see-**koo**-roh pahr-keh-jyah-reh kwee

DIRECTIONS

Is this the road (way) to...?	È questa la strada per...?	eh **kweh**-stah lah **strah**-dah pehr
Are we on the right road for...?	Siamo sulla strada giusta per...?	**syah**-moh sool-lah strah-dah **joo**-stah pehr
I think I'm lost.	Penso che mi sono perso.	**pehn**-soh keh mee **soh**-(-ah)
Please, show me where are we on the map?	Può indicarmi dove siamo sulla carta?	**pwoh** een-dee-**kahr**-mee **doh**-veh **syah**-moh **sool**-lah **kahr**-tah
Excuse me, how do I get to...?	Mi scusi, come potrei raggiungere la strada per...?	mee skoo-zee, **koh**-meh poh-**tray** rah-**jyoon**-jeh-reh lah strah-dah pehr
In what direction?	In che direzione devo andare?	een keh dee-reh-**tsyoh**-neh **deh**-voh ahn-**dah**-reh

Right?	A destra?	ah **dehs**-trah
Left?	A sinistra?	ah see-**nees**-trah
Straight ahead?	Sempre diritto?	**sehm**-preh dee-**reet**-toh
To the traffic light?	Al semaforo?	ahl seh-**mah**-foh-roh
To the next corner?	Al prossimo angolo?	ahl **prohs**-see-moh **ahn**-goh-loh
How long does it take by car?	Quanto ci vuole in macchina?	**kwahn**-toh chee voo-**oh**-leh een **mahk**-kee-nah
What is this place called?	Dove siamo?	**doh**-veh see-**ah**-moh

GAS STATION

Where is the next gas station?	Dov'è la prossima stazione di servizio?	dohv-**eh** lah **prohs**-see-mah stah-**tsyoh**-neh dee sehr-**vee**-tsyoh
Give me 45 litres.	Mi dia quaranta cinque litri.	mee **dee**-ah kwah-**rahn**-tah **cheen**-kweh **lee**-tree
Fill it up with...	*Faccia il pieno di...*	***fah**-chyah eel **pyeh**-noh dee*
diesel	diesel	**dee**-sehl
regular	normale	nohr-**mah**-leh
super	super	**soo**-pehr
Check the...	*Per favore mi controlli...*	*pehr fah-voh-reh mee kohn-trohl-lee*
antifreeze	l'acqua	**lah**-kwah
battery	la batteria	lah baht-teh-**ree**-ah
brakes	i freni	ee **freh**-nee
oil	l'olio	**loh**-lee-oh
spark plugs	le candele	leh kahn-**deh**-leh
tire pressure	la pressione delle gomme	lah prehs-**syoh**-neh **dehl**-leh **gohm**-meh

CAR PROBLEMS

I have run out of gas.	Sono senza benzina.	**soh**-noh **sehn**-zah behn-**zee**-nah
I've left the keys inside the car.	Ho lasciato le chiavi in macchina.	oh lah-**shah**-toh leh **kyah**-vee een **mahk**-kee-nah

My car has broken down.	Mi si è guastata la macchina.	mee see eh gwah-**stah**-tah lah **mahk**-kee-nah
Where can I find a mechanic?	Ho bisogno di un meccanico.	oh bee-**zoh**-nyoh dee oon mehk-**kah**-nee-koh
Can you tow the car to the nearest garage?	Può rimorchiare la macchina al garage più vicino?	**pwoh** ree-mohr-**kyah**-reh lah **mahk**-kee-nah ahl gah-**rahj** pyoo vee-**chee**-noh
The motor doesn't start.	La macchina non si mette in moto/non parte.	lah **mahk**-kee-nah nohn see **meht**-teh een **moh**-toh/nohn **pahr**-teh
Please check the...	*Per favore, mi controlli...*	*pehr fah-**voh**-reh, mee kohn-**trohl**-lee*
battery	la batteria	lah baht-teh-**ree**-ah
brake lights	i fari posteriori	ee **fah**-ree poh-steh-**ryoh**-ree
brakes	i freni	ee **freh**-nee
clutch	la frizione	lah free-**tsyoh**-neh
fan belt	la cinghia del ventilatore	lah **cheen**-ghyah dehl vehn-tee-lah-**toh**-reh
gearshift	il cambio	eel **kahm**-byoh
headlights	i fari anteriori	ee **fah**-ree ahn-teh-**ryoh**-ree
ignition	l'accensione	lah-chehn-**syoh**-neh
motor	il motore	eel moh-**toh**-reh
oil	l'olio	**loh**-lee-oh
tire pressure	la pressione delle gomme	lah prehs-**syoh**-neh **dehl**-leh **gohm**-meh
tires	le gomme	leh **gohm**-meh
I have a flat tire/ puncture.	Ho una gomma bucata.	oh oo-nah **gohm**-mah boo-**kah**-tah
Change this tire.	Mi cambi questa ruota.	mee **kahm**-bee **kweh**-stah **rwoh**-tah
Can you fix this?	La può riparare?	lah **pwoh** ree-pah-**rah**-reh
How much will it cost?	Quanto costerà?	**kwahn**-toh koh-steh-**rah**
Do you have the part?	Ha il pezzo di ricambio?	**ah**-ee eel **peht**-tsoh dee ree-**kahm**-byoh

How long will it take?	Quanto tempo ci vorrà?	**kwahn**-toh **tehm**-poh chee vohr-**rah**
How much do I owe you?	Quanto le devo?	**kwahn**-toh leh **deh**-voh
Thank you very much.	Grazie mille.	**grah**-tsyeh **meel**-leh

What you may hear

Possibilmente...	*Possibly for...*
per domani	tomorrow
per dopo domani	the day after tomorrow
stasera	this evening
Possiamo fare un riparazione provvisoria.	We can fix it temporarily.
È impossibile oggi.	It's impossible today.
Non abbiamo i pezzi di ricambio.	We don't have the parts.
Verrà a costare...lire.	It will cost...lira.

BORDER FORMALITIES

Whether travelling by car, train or boat, most of the questions posed by customs officials will be the same. Have your papers ready and in order.

Here is my passport.	Ecco il mio passaporto.	**ehk**-koh eel **mee**-oh pahs-sah-**pohr**-toh
Here is my license.	Ecco la mia patente internazionale.	**ehk**-koh lah **mee**-ah pah-**tehn**-teh

When in doubt

Excuse me!	Chiedo scusa.	**kyeh**-doh **skoo**-zah
I'm Canadian.	Sono canadese.	**soh**-noh kah-nah-**deh**-zeh
I don't speak Italian.	Non parlo italiano.	nohn **pahr**-loh ee-tah-**lyah**-noh
I'm lost.	Non so dove mi trovo.	nohn soh **doh**-veh mee **troh**-voh
I need a translator.	Ho bisogno di un interprete.	oh bee-**zoh**-nyoh dee oon een-**tehr**-preh-teh

What you may hear

Per favore,...	*Please show me...*
il passaporto	your passport
la patente di guida	car documents

Ha qualcosa da dichiarare?	Do you have any thing to declare?
Può aprire...	*Please open...*
le valigie	this suitcase
il portabagagli	the trunk
Sono effetti personali?	Are these your things?
Bisogna pagare la dogana.	You must pay the duty at the cashier.

TRAIN TRAVEL

There are many types of trains in Italy. When buying tickets for train travel, be sure to specify what type of train you would like. The **E.C. - Eurocity** are first-class, luxury express trains. You will need a reservation and a seat supplement is added to the cost of the ticket. The **I.C. - Intercity** offers direct service between major cities. Luxury, first and second class are available with a fare supplements for seat reservations. The **Pendolino** is the newest, bullet train. The **Rapido** is also an express train. Reservations, seat supplement are compulsory. The **Espresso** is a long-distance train and makes few stops. The **Diretto** is operated as a shorter-distance train and stops at major stations. The **Locale/Accelerato** is the local train and stops at most stations.

Italian train schedules use the 24-hour clock. Check your tickets carefully.

SIGN LANGUAGE

AI TRENI	TO THE TRAINS	**ah**-ee **treh**-nee
ALT!	STOP!	**ahlt**
ACQUA (NON) POTABILE	(NOT) POTABLE WATER	**ah**-kwah (nohn) poh-**tah**-bee-leh
ARRIVI	ARRIVALS	ahr-**ree**-vee
BAGAGLI	BAGGAGE CLAIM	bah-**gah**-lyee
BAGAGLIAIO	LUGGAGE CAR	bah-gah-**lyah**-yoh
BIGLIETTERIA	TICKET OFFICE	bee-lyeh-teh-**ree**-ah

SIGN LANGUAGE

BINARIO	PLATFORM, TRACK	bee-**nah**-ree-oh
CALDO (C)	HOT (WATER)	**kahl**-doh
CARROZZA RISTORANTE	(RESTAURANT) DINING CAR	kah-**roht**-tsah ree-stoh-**rahn**-teh
FREDDO (F)	COLD (WATER)	**frehd**-doh
PERICOLO!	DANGER!	peh-**ree**-koh-loh
RITIRATA	W.C. (TRAINS)	ree-tee-**rah**-tah
SALA D'ATTESA	WAITING AREA (HALL)	**sah**-lah daht-**teh**-zah
SIGNORE, DONNE	WOMEN (TOILET)	see-**nyoh**-reh, **dohn**-neh
SIGNORI, UOMINI	MEN (TOILET)	**woh**-mee-nee
SPINGERE	PUSH	**speen**-jeh-reh
TIRARE	PULL	tee-**rah**-reh
UFFICIO OGGETTI SMARRITI	LOST & FOUND OFFICE	oof-**fee**-chyoh ohj-**jeht**-tee smah-**ree**-tee
UFFICIO INFORMAZIONI	INQUIRY DESK	oof-**fee**-chyoh een-fohr-mah-**tsyoh**-nee
USCITA	EXIT	oo-**shee**-tah
USCITA DI EMERGENZA	EMERGENCY EXIT	oo-**shee**-tah dee eh-mehr-**jehn**-zah
VAGONE	CAR	vah-**goh**-neh
VIETATO FUMARE	NO SMOKING	vyeh-**tah**-toh foo-**mah**-reh
VIETATO ENTRARE	NO ENTRANCE	vyeh-**tah**-toh ehn-**trah**-reh
VIETATO USCIRE	NO EXIT	vyeh-**tah**-toh oo-**shee**-reh

Where is the train station?	Dov'è la stazione ferroviaria?	dohv-**eh** lah stah-**tsyoh**-neh fehr-roh-**vyah**-re-ah
I'd like one ticket (two, three tickets)...	*Vorrei un biglietto (due, tre biglietti)...*	*vohr-**ray** oon bee-**lyeht**-toh (doo-eh, treh bee-**lyeht**-tee)*
with reserved seating	con prenotazione	kohn preh-noh-tah-**tsyoh**-neh

first-class	di prima classe	dee **pree**-mah **klahs**-seh
first-class sleeping car	il vagone letto	eel vah-**goh**-neh **leht**-toh
second-class	di seconda classe	dee seh-**kohn**-dah **klahs**-seh
second-class sleeping car	le cuccette	leh koo-**cheht**-teh
return trip	di andata e ritorno	dee ahn-**dah**-tah eh ree-**tohr**-noh
one way	di andata	dee ahn-**dah**-tah
with supplement for the rapid train	con supplemento rapido	kohn soo-plee-**mehn**-toh **rah**-pee-doh
I'd like the smoking car.	Vorrei il scompartimento ai fumatori.	vohr-**ray** eel skohm-pahr-tee-**mehn**-toh **ah**-ee foo-mah-**toh**-ree
I'd like the non-smoking car.	Vorrei il scompartimento ai non fumatori.	vohr-**ray** eel skohm-pahr-tee-**mehn**-toh **ah**-ee nohn foo-mah-**toh**-ree
How much is the ticket?	Quanto costa il biglietto?	**kwahn**-toh **koh**-stah eel bee-**lyeht**-toh
The train is on time/ late.	Il treno è in orario/in ritardo.	eel **treh**-noh eh een oh-**rah**-ree-oh/een ree-**tahr**-doh
Where is the luggage check?	Dov'è il deposito bagagli?	dohv-**eh** eel dee-**poh**-zee-toh bah-**gah**-lyee
Where is the lost and found?	Dov'è l'ufficio oggetti smarriti?	dohv-**eh** loof-**fee**-chyoh ohj-**jeh**-tee smah-**ree**-tee
Which train do I take to get to..	Che treno devo prendere per andare a...?	keh **treh**-noh **deh**-voh **prehn**-deh-reh ah
From what platform does the train leave?	Da che binario parte il treno?	dah keh bee-**nah**-ree-oh **pahr**-teh eel **treh**-noh

Assistance

I need a porter.	Ho bisogno di un bagagliaio.	oh bee-**zoh**-nyoh dee oon bah-gah-**lyah**-yoh
Here is my luggage.	Ecco le valigie.	**ehk**-koh leh vah-**lee**-jyeh
Be careful, please.	Stia attento, per favore.	**stee**-ah aht-**tehn**-toh pehr fah-**voh**-reh
Please put my things here.	Per favore, mi mette qui.	pehr fah-**voh**-reh mee **meht**-teh kwee

Making Sure!

Does this train stop at...?	Questo treno si ferme a...?	**kweh**-stoh **treh**-noh see **fehr**-meh ah
When does the train depart for...?	Quando parte il treno per...?	**kwahn**-doh **pahr**-teh eel **treh**-noh pehr
When does the train arrive at...?	Quando arriva il treno a...?	**kwahn**-doh ahr-**ree**-vah eel **treh**-noh ah
How long does it stop here?	Quanto tempo si ferma?	**kwahn**-toh **tehm**-poh see **fehr**-mah
Is there time to grab a bite?	C'è tempo per comprare un boccone?	cheh **tehm**-poh pehr kohm-**prah**-reh oon bohk-**koh**-neh
Is there a dining car?	C'è un vagone ristorante?	cheh oon vah-**goh**-neh ree-stoh-**rahn**-teh
Is there a sleeping car?	C'è un vagone letto?	cheh oon vah-**goh**-neh **leht**-toh
Is it an express/local train?	È un treno rapido/ locale?	eh oon **treh**-noh **rah**-pee-doh/loh-**kah**-leh
Do I have to change trains?	Debbo cambiare treno?	**dehb**-boh kahm-**byah**-reh **treh**-noh

Problems

Excuse me, but you are in my seat.	Mi scusi ma lei ha occupato il mio posto.	mee **skoo**-see mah **leh**-ee ah ohk-koo-**pah**-toh eel **mee**-oh **poh**-stoh
Can you please help me?	Può aiutarmi?	**pwoh** ah-yoo-**tahr**-mee
I can't find my ticket.	Non trovo il mio biglietto.	nohn **troh**-voh eel mee-oh bee-**lyeht**-toh
I took the wrong train.	Ho sbagliato il treno.	oh zbah-**lyah**-toh eel **treh**-noh
We have missed the train.	Abbiamo perso il treno.	ahb-**byah**-moh **pehr**-soh eel **treh**-noh
When is the next train?	Quando arriva il prossimo treno?	**kwahn**-doh ahr-**ree**-vah eel **prohs**-see-moh **treh**-noh

CHAPTER ELEVEN

Medical and emergency phrases

Help (me)!	Aiuto!	ah-**yoo**-toh
I'm ill.	Sto male.	stoh **mah**-leh
I don't feel well.	Non mi sento bene.	nonh mee **sehn**-toh **beh**-neh
I feel weak.	Mi sento debole.	mee **sehn**-toh **deh**-boh-leh
I feel dizzy.	Mi gira la testa.	mee **jee**-rah lah **teh**-stah
I need a doctor quickly!	Ho bisogno urgente del medico.	oh bee-**zoh**-nyoh oor-**jehn**-teh dehl **meh**-dee-koh
Please call...	*Per favore, chiamate...*	*pehr fah-**voh**-reh, kyah-**mah**-teh*
a doctor	un medico	oon **meh**-dee-koh
an ambulance	un'ambulanza	oon ahm-boo-**lahn**-tsah
Does the doctor speak English?	Il dottore parla inglese?	eel doht-**toh**-reh **pahr**-lah een-**gleh**-zeh
Will the doctor come to the hotel?	Il dottore potrà venire all'hotel?	eel doht-**toh**-reh poh-**trah** veh-**nee**-reh ahl-oh-**tehl**
When can the doctor come?	Quando può venire?	**kwahn**-doh **pwoh** veh-**nee**-reh
Please, as soon as possible.	Per piacere, più presto possibile.	pehr pyah-**cheh**-reh pyoo **preh**-stoh pohs-**see**-bee-leh

Accidents

He (she) fainted.	È svenuto (-a).	eh zveh-**noo**-toh (-tah)
I've had an accident.	Ho avuto un incidente.	oh ah-**voo**-toh oon een-chee-**dehn**-teh
I think I've had a heart attack.	Credo che ho avuto un collasso cardiaco.	**kreh**-doh keh oh ah-**voo**-toh oon kohl-**lahs**-soh kahr-**dee**-ah-koh
Call an ambulance!	Chiamate un'ambulanza!	kyah-**mah**-teh oon ahm-boo-**lahn**-tsah
Take me to a hospital!	Mi porti all'ospedale!	mee **pohr**-tee ahl-oh-speh-**dah**-leh
I need first aid fast!	Ho bisogno di pronto soccorso. È urgente!	oh bee-**zoh**-nyoh dee **prohn**-toh sohk-**kohr**-soh. eh oor-jehn-teh

BEFORE YOU CALL!

An attempt has been made to cover many situations. If possible, have someone with you when you call. If you call from your hotel room, you will be asked some of the following questions.

What you may hear

Il numero della vostra camera?	eel **noo**-meh-roh **dehl**-lah voh-strah **kah**-meh-rah	(What's) your room number?
Che sintomi ha?	keh seen-**toh**-mee ah	What's wrong with you?
Dove fa male?	**doh**-veh fah **mah**-leh	Where does it hurt?

If you can, have your answer ready.

I don't speak Italian.	Non parlo italiano.	nohn **pahr**-loh eet-ah-**lyah**-noh
When can the doctor come?	Quando può venire il dottore?	**kwahn**-doh **pwoh** veh-**nee**-reh eel doht-**toh**-reh
This is my medicine.	Questa è la medicina che prendo.	**kweh**-stah eh lah meh-dee-**chee**-nah keh **prehn**-doh

I'm (not) allergic to...	*(Non) sono allergico...*	*(nohn)* ***soh****-noh ahl-****lehr****-jee-koh*
antibiotics	agli antibiotici	**ah**-lyee ahn-tee-bee-**oh**-tee-chee
penicillin	alla penicillina	**ahl**-lah pehn-nee-cheel-**lee**-nah
sulfa	ai sulfamidici	**ah**-ee sool-fah-**meh**-dee-chee
certain medicines	a certe medicine	ah **chehr**-teh meh-dee-**chee**-neh
Does the doctor speak English?	Il dottore parla inglese?	eel doht-**toh**-reh **pahr**-lah een-**gleh**-zeh

What's wrong?

I've got...	*Ho...*	*oh*
asthma	l'asma	**lahz**-mah
angina	l'angina	lahn-**ghee**-nah
high blood pressure	il pressione alto	eel prehs-**syoh**-neh **ahl**-toh
low blood pressure	il pressione basso	eel prehs-**syoh**-neh **bahs**-soh
I'm diabetic.	Ho il diabete.	oh eel dee-ah-**beh**-teh
I've had a heart attack...	*Ho avuto un attacco cardiaco...*	*oh ah-****voo****-toh oon aht-****tahk****-koh kahr-****dee****-ah-koh*
last year	l'anno scorso	**lahn**-noh **skohr**-soh
(three) years ago	(tre) anni fa	(treh) **ahn**-nee fah
I'm pregnant.	Sono incinta.	**soh**-noh een-**cheen**-tah
It hurts here (point).	Mi fa male qui.	mee fah **mah**-leh kwee

For quick reference, these are listed alphabetically in English.

I have (a, an)...	*Ho...*	*oh...*
abscess	un ascesso	oon ah-**shehs**-soh
asthma	l'asma	**lahz**-mah
bite	preso un morso	**preh**-zoh oon **mohr**-soh
burn	una bruciatura	**oo**-nah broo-chyah-**too**-rah

I have (a, an)...	*Ho...*	*oh...*
chest pain	un dolore nel petto	oon doh-**loh**-reh nehl **peht**-toh
constipation	la stitichezza	lah stee-tee-**keht**-tsah
cough	la tosse	lah **tohs**-seh
diarrhea	la diarrea	lah dee-ah-**reh**-ah
fever	la febbre	lah **fehb**-breh
flu	l'influenza	leen-floo-**ehn**-zah
food poisoning	un'intossicazione da cibo	oon een-tohs-see-kah-**tsyoh**-neh dah **chee**-boh
gastric pain	i crampi allo stomaco	ee **krahm**-pee **ahl**-loh **stoh**-mah-koh
head cold	un raffreddore	oon rahf-frehd-**doh**-reh
high blood pressure	la pressione alto	lah prehs-**syoh**-neh **ahl**-toh
insomnia	l'insomnia	leen-**sohm**-nee-ah
low blood pressure	la pressione basso	lah prehs-**syoh**-neh **bahs**-soh
nausea	la nausea	lah **now**-zeh-ah
pain in the back	i dolori nella schiena	ee doh-**loh**-ree **nehl**-lah **skyeh**-nah
a sting	una puntura d'insetto	**oo**-nah poon-**too**-rah deen-**seht**-toh
swelling	un gonfiore	oon gohn-**fyoh**-reh
wound (cut)	una ferita (un taglio)	**oo**-nah feh-**ree**-tah (oon **tah**-lyoh)

It hurts...

I have (my... hurts).	*Mi fa male...*	*mee fah mah-leh*
chest pain	il petto	eel **peht**-toh
head	la testa	lah **teh**-stah
sore back	la schiena	lah **skyeh**-nah
sore throat	la gola	lah **goh**-lah
stomachache	lo stomaco	loh **stoh**-mah-koh
I have menstrual pain.	Ho dolori mestruali.	oh doh-**loh**-ree meh-stroo-**ah**-lee

EXAMINATION

What you may be asked

Mi dica dove Le fa male?	mee **dee**-kah **doh**-veh leh fah **mah**-leh	Where does it hurt?
Respiri profondamente.	reh-**spee**-ree proh-fohn-dah-**mehn**-teh	Breathe deeply.
Respiri normalmente.	reh-**spee**-ree nohr-mahl-**mehn**-teh	Breathe normally.
Le misuro la febbre/ la pressione.	leh mee-**zoo**-roh lah **fehb**-breh	I'll take your temperature /pressure.
Da quanto tempo soffre di questi disturbi?	dah **kwahn**-toh **tehm**-poh **sohf**-freh dee **kweh**-stee dee-**stoor**-bee	How long have you had these pains?
Come si senta oggi?	**koh**-meh see **sehn**-teh **ohj**-jee	How are you feeling today?
Si spogli (fino alla vita).	see **spoh**-lyee (**fee**-noh **ahl**-lah **vee**-tah)	Get undressed (to the waist).
Si sdrai.	see **zdrah**-ee	Lie down.
Non respiri.	nohn reh-**spee**-ree	Hold your breath.
Si vesta.	see **veh**-stah	Get dressed.
Apra la bocca.	**ah**-prah lah **bohk**-kah	Open your mouth.
Faccia vedere la lingua.	**fah**-chyah veh-**deh**-reh lah **leen**-gwah	Show (me) your tongue.
Tossisca.	tohs-**see**-skah	Cough.
Cosa avete mangiato?	**koh**-zah ah-**veh**-teh mahn-**jyah**-toh	What did you eat?

AT THE PHARMACY

Where is the pharmacy?	Dov'è la farmacia?	dohv-**eh** lah fahr-mah-**chee**-ah
Is there a pharmacy near here?	C'è una farmacia qui vicino?	cheh **oo**-nah fahr-mah-**chee**-ah kwee vee-**chee**-noh
Is there an all-night pharmacy?	C'è una farmacia di turno?	cheh **oo**-nah fahr-mah-**chee**-ah dee **toor**-noh
What time does the pharmacy open/close?	A che ora apre/chiude la farmacia?	ah keh **oh**-rah **ah**-preh/ **kyoo**-deh lah fahr-mah-**chee**-ah

I (don't) have a prescription.	(Non) ho la ricetta.	(nohn) oh lah ree-**cheht**-tah

MINI-DICTIONARY

Please, I need something for (a, an)...	*Ho bisogno di qualcosa per...*	*oh bee-**zoh**-nyoh dee kwahl-**koh**-zah pehr*
burn	la bruciatura	lah broo-chyah-**too**-rah
car (motion) sickness	il mal d'auto	eel mahl **dow**-toh
cold	il raffreddore	eel rahf-freh-**doh**-reh
constipation	la stitichezza	lah stee-tee-**keht**-tsah
corns	i calli	ee **kahl**-lee
cough	la tosse	lah **tohs**-seh
diarrhea	la diarrea	lah dee-ah-**reh**-ah
fever	la febbre	lah **fehb**-breh
hay fever	una rinite da fieno	**oo**-nah ree-**nee**-teh dah **fyeh**-noh
headache	il mal di testa	eel mahl dee **teh**-stah
indigestion	l'indigestione	leen-dee-jeh-**styoh**-neh
seasickness	il mal di mare	eel mahl dee **mah**-reh
stomachache	il mal di stomaco	eel mahl dee **stoh**-mah-koh
sunburn	la scottatura solare	lah skoht-tah-**too**-rah soh-**lah**-reh
throat ache	il mal di gola	eel mal dee **goh**-lah
toothache	il mal di dente	eel mahl dee **dehn**-teh
I would like a, an (some)...	*Vorrei...*	*vohr-ray*
(mild) laxative	un lassativo (leggero)	oon lahs-sah-**tee**-voh (leh-**jeh**-roh)
antacid	un antiacido	oon ahn-tee-**ah**-chee-doh
antiseptic	del'antisettico	dehl ahn-tee-**seht**-tee-koh
aspirin	dell'aspirina	dehl ah-spee-**ree**-nah
bandages	dei cerotti	**deh**-ee cheh-**roht**-tee
contact lens cleaner	del detergente per lenti a contatto	dehl deh-tehr-**jehn**-teh pehr **lehn**-tee ah kohn-**tah**-toh
corn plasters	dei callifughi	**deh**-ee kahl-lee-**foo**-ghee

cotton balls	del cotone idrofilo	dehl koh-**toh**-neh ee-droh-**fee**-loh
cough syrup	dello sciroppo per la tosse	**dehl**-loh shee-**rohp**-poh pehr lah **tohs**-seh
cough drops	delle pastiglie per la tosse	**dehl**-leh pah-**stee**-lyeh pehr lah **tohs**-seh
ear drops	delle gocce per gli orecchi	**dehl**-leh **goh**-cheh pehr lyee oh-**rehk**-kee
eye drops	del collirio	dehl kohl-**lee**-ree-oh
iodine	della tintura di iodio	**deh**-lah teen-**too**-rah dee ee-**oh**-dee-oh
mouthwash	del collutorio	dehl kohl-loo-**toh**-ree-oh
prophylactics	dei preservativi, profilattici	**deh**-ee preh-sehr-vah-**tee**-vee, proh-fee-**lah**-tee-chee
sanitary napkins	degli assorbenti igienici	**deh**-lyee ahs-sor-**behn**-tee ee-**jyeh**-nee-chee
tampons	dei tamponi	**deh**-ee tahm-**poh**-nee
vitamins	delle vitamine	**dehl**-leh vee-tah-**mee**-nee
How much does it cost?	Quanto costa?	**kwahn**-toh **koh**-stah

AT THE DENTIST

I have...	*Ho...*	*oh*
a toothache	il mal di denti	eel mahl dee **dehn**-tee
lost a filling	perduto l'otturazione	pehr-**doo**-toh loht-too-rah-**tsyoh**-neh
I've broken my...	*Mi si è rotta...*	*mee see eh* ***roht****-tah*
denture	la dentiera	lah dehn-**tyeh**-rah
crown	la corona	lah koh-**roh**-nah
I have broken my bridge.	Mi si è rotto il ponte.	mee see eh **roht**-toh eel **pohn**-teh
I have sore gums.	Mi fanno male le gengive.	mee **fahn**-noh mah-leh leh jehn-**jee**-veh
I've broken a tooth.	Mi son rotto un dente.	mee sohn **roht**-toh oon **dehn**-teh
Is there an infection?	C'è un'infezione?	cheh oon een-feh-**tsyoh**-neh

I need to see a dentist.	Devo andare al dentista.	**deh**-voh ahn-**dah**-reh ahl dehn-**tee**-stah
Can you fix it...?	*Lo può otturare...?*	*loh* ***pwoh*** *oht-too-***rah***-reh*
with amalgam	con l'algama	kohn lahl-**gah**-mah
with gold	con oro	kohn **oh**-roh
with silver	con argento	kohn ahr-**jehn**-toh
temporarily	provvisoriamente	proh-vee-soh-ryah-**mehn**-teh
I don't want it pulled out.	Non lo voglio togliere.	nonh loh **voh**-lyoh **toh**-lyeh-reh
I want a local anesthetic.	Vorrei l'anestesia locale.	**vohr**-ray lah-neh-steh-**zee**-ah loh-**kah**-leh
Stop. It still hurts.	Ferma! Mi fa male.	**fehr**-mah mee fah **mah**-leh
When will it be ready?	Quando sarà pronta?	**kwahn**-doh **sah**-rah **prohn**-tah
How much do I owe you for your services?	Quanto le devo per la visita?	**kwahn**-toh leh **deh**-voh pehr lah **vee**-zee-tah
When should I come back?	Quando dovrei ritornare?	**kwahn**-doh dohv-**ray** ree-tohr-**nah**-reh
Can I have the receipt?	Mi può fare una ricevuta?	mee **pwoh** **fah**-reh oo-nah ree-che-**voo**-tah

What you may hear

Le fa male?	leh fah **mah**-leh	Does it hurt?
Qual dente fa male?	kwahl **dehn**-teh fah **mah**-leh	Which tooth hurts?
Apra la bocca.	**ah**-prah lah **bohk**-kah	Open your mouth.
Ritorni domani, fra (qualche)...giorni.	ree-**tohr**-nee doh-**mah**-nee, frah (**kwahl**-keh) ...**jyohr**-nee	Come and see me tomorrow, in (a few)... days.
Abbiamo finito.	ahb-**byah**-moh fee-**nee**-toh	We're finished.

POLICE MATTERS & OTHER EMERGENCIES

Help!	Aiuto!	ah-**yoo**-toh
Fire!	Al fuoco!	ahl **fwoh**-koh
Thief.	Ladro!	**lah**-droh
Stop him!	Fermatelo!	fehr-**mah**-teh-loh
Call the police.	Chiami la polizia.	**kyah**-mee lah poh-lee-**tsee**-yah
I've lost my...	*Ho perso...*	*oh* ***pehr****-soh...*
They've stolen my...	*Mi hanno rubato...*	*mee* ***ahn****-noh roo-****bah****-toh*
camera	la macchina fotografica	lah **mahk**-kee-nah foh-toh-**grah**-fee-kah
car keys	le chiavi della macchina	leh **kyah**-vee **dehl**-lah **mahk**-kee-nah
credit cards	le carte di credito	leh **kahr**-teh dee **kreh**-dee-toh
handbag	la borsetta	lah bohr-**seht**-tah
money	i soldi	ee **sohl**-dee
passport	il passaporto	eel pahs-sah-**pohr**-toh
suitcase	la valigia	lah vah-**lee**-jyah
wallet	il portafoglio	eel pohr-tah-**foh**-lyoh
watch	l'orologio	lohr-oh-**loh**-jyoh

You will often see local women walking arm in arm or holding hands. This gives men a clear "don't hassle me" message.

What you may need to say!

Leave me alone.	Mi lasci in pace.	mee **lah**-shee een **pah**-cheh
Don't touch me.	Non mi tocchi.	nohn mee **tohk**-kee
Enough!	Basta!	**bah**-stah
This man is following me.	Questo uomo mi segue.	**kweh**-stoh **woh**-moh mee **seh**-gweh
I'll call the police.	Chiamo la polizia.	**kyah**-moh lah poh-lee-**stee**-yah

Emergency Card

A crisis can reduce us to babbling unintelligibly even in our first language. Dealing with serious problems in a language we are just "trying on" is more stressful still. This is why we recommend that you complete this emergency card and keep a copy in your wallet with your ID.

Name: ______________________________
first name/surname (nome/\cognome)

Address : ______________________________
number/street (indirizzo)

____
city/postal code/province (città\provincia)

Telephone number: ______________________________
telephone number (numero di telefono)

Blood group (gruppo di sangue) ______________________________

Health card number
(numero di carta di santità) ______________________________

Medical insurance company and policy number
(assicurazione e numero della polizza): ______________________________

Traveller's insurance company and policy number
(assicurazione di viaggio): ______________________________

Date of last tetanus shot
(ultimo iniezione di tetano): ______________________________

Allergies (allergie): ______________________________

Other medical conditions
(altri condizione medicali): ______________________________

Medication (medicine): ______________________________

Person to contact in case of emergency:
(in caso di emergenza):

Name: ______________________________
first name/surname (nome/\cognome)

Address: ______________________________
number/street (indirizzo)

____
city/postal code/province (città\provincia)

Telephone number: ______________________________
telephone number (numero di telefono) fax

NOTES & UPDATES